Iceland

Iceland

BY BARBARA A. SOMERVILL

Enchantment of the World
Second Series

Children's Press®

A Division of Scholastic Inc.

NEW YORK TORONTO LONDON AUCKLAND SYDNEY
MEXICO CITY NEW DELHI HONG KONG
DANBURY, CONNECTICUT

Frontispiece: A small boat floats among icebergs in Jokulsarian Lagoon

Consultant: Dr. Patricia Conroy, Associate Professor, Department of Scandinavian Studies, University of Washington, Seattle

Please note: All statistics are as up-to-date as possible at the time of publication.

Book production by Herman Adler Design

Library of Congress Cataloging-in-Publication Data

Somervill, Barbara A.
    Iceland / by Barbara A. Somervill
        p. cm. — (Enchantment of the world. Second series)
    Includes bibliographical references and index.
    ISBN 0-516-22694-0
    1. Iceland—Juvenile literature. I. Title. II. Series.
DL305 .S66 2002
949.12—dc21   2002001644

Acknowledgments

A sincere thank you to the Icelandic Tourist Bureau, the *Iceland Review*, the Icelandic Embassy, and the many people of Iceland who responded to the author's request for information about Iceland and its people.

Cover photo:
Rock outcroppings
on Lake Mývatn

Contents

CHAPTER

Icelandic horse

An Icelandic girl

Þorri breathed a sigh of relief. He had finally finished months of study for his confirmation at Akureyrikirkja, the large Lutheran church in Akureyri where he lives. Last Wednesday, the class had rehearsed for the Easter ceremony in which Þorri and his friends would participate.

Confirmation is a rite of passage for Icelandic youths, and most children participate. In all, eleven fourteen-year-olds are in Þorri's class. Like most Icelandic children of his age, Þorri has looked forward to the ceremony—but has hated the months of classes that took him away from soccer games and swimming in the city's heated pool.

On Saturday, Þorri and his mother, Hanna, flew to Reykjavík, Iceland's capital city, on a shuttle airplane. The trip from Akureyri to the capital only took forty-five minutes by air but would have been a long five-hour drive by car. Þorri and Hanna shopped in the Kringlan, an indoor shopping mall near the new city center. They bought a navy pin-stripe suit, a blue oxford-cloth shirt, and black dress shoes for Þorri to wear at the ceremony. Hanna grit her teeth as Þorri picked out a wild-patterned tie to complete the outfit, but she finally agreed to let him buy it.

Opposite: **After months of preparing, these Icelandic teens have participated in their confirmation ceremony.**

Shopping at the Kringlan mall

Reading Icelandic

Like many other languages, Icelandic has some letter combinations that are not used in English. This key will help you pronounce the Icelandic names and words in this book.

Þ	the sound of "th," as in "thud"
ð	the sound of "th," as in "mother"
J, j	the sound of "y," as in "you"
Æ, æ	the sound of "ai," as in "rain"
Ö, ö	the sound of "uh," as in "the"
Ó, ó	the sound of "o," as in "hope"
Í, í, Ý, ý	the sound of "ee," as in "free"
Á, á	the sound of "o," as in "how"
É, é	the sound of "ee-eh," as in "pizzeria"
Ú, ú	the sound of "oo," as in "boo"

Þorri's entire family plans to attend the church service. After the ceremony, there will be a party for family, friends, and neighbors. Hanna has plenty to do to prepare for the party. She will serve a buffet supper, including many traditional Icelandic dishes: fish balls, smoked cod, and potatoes in cream gravy. A celebration dinner might also include the national dish, called *hangikjöt* (smoked mutton). Guests would also enjoy *hákard* (aged shark).

Traditional Icelandic food is served buffet style.

Þorri's sister, Kalli, helps out in the kitchen by making sand cakes, a popular treat. His grandmother Sigga has a reputation for baking excellent *flatbrauð* (flatbread) and *kleinur* (a type of doughnut). Kalli and Sigga promise to do the baking if Hanna does all the other cooking.

Easter comes early this year, and March weather in Akureyri is often severe. Bad winter weather is no surprise because the city is only about 60 miles (100 kilometers) south of the Arctic Circle. Þorri's confirmation day is no exception. Strong winds and wet snow make driving treacherous.

An eiderdown quilt for cold Icelandic nights

Þorri's parents and sister sit with his grandparents, aunt, and uncle near the front of the church. When the ceremony begins, Þorri and the others in his class march down the center aisle, dressed in long white robes. The minister offers a sermon on the responsibilities of adulthood as part of the ceremony. When the minister calls, "Þorsteinn Ragnar Einarsson," Þorri steps forward to be confirmed. It's over!

At home, friends and neighbors drop by to congratulate Þorri on his step toward adulthood. Confirmation is a major gift-giving event, and Þorri receives many presents. His grandparents give him an eiderdown quilt, a traditional gift that he

Modern technology is commonly used in Iceland.

will keep all his life. His parents give him a laptop computer—the perfect gift for a gadget-mad Icelandic teenager. Hanna and Einar hope he'll use it for schoolwork; Þorri plans to play computer games and set up an e-mail address. Kalli gives him books, a popular gift in Iceland, where more books are published per person than in any other country on Earth.

The day finally ends. Þorri and his family are exhausted. He leans over and kisses his mother's cheek. *"Takk fyrir, Mama,"* he says. "Thank you very much, Mom."

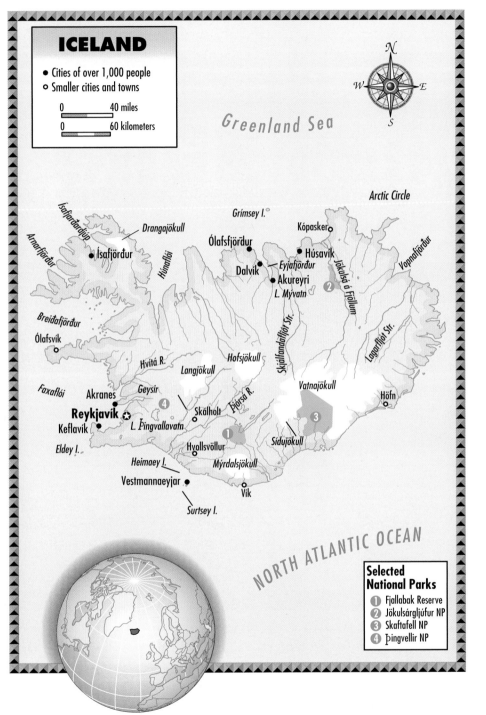

ICELAND

- Cities of over 1,000 people
- Smaller cities and towns

0   40 miles

0   60 kilometers

Greenland Sea

N
W   E
S

Arctic Circle

Ísafjarðardjúp

Drangajökull

Grímsey I.

Kópasker

Ólafsfjörður

Húsavík

Arnarfjörður

Ísafjörður

Húnaflói

Dalvík

Eyjafjörður

Akureyri

L. Mývatn

Jökulsá á Fjöllum

Vopnafjörður

Breiðafjörður

Skjálfandafljót Str.

Lagarfljót Str.

Ólafsvík

Hofsjökull

Hvítá R.

Langjökull

Vatnajökull

Faxaflói

Akranes

Geysir

Þjórsá R.

Höfn

Reykjavik

Skálholt

④

Keflavík

L. Þingvallavatn

①

③

Eldey I.

Hvollsvöllur

Síðujökull

Heimaey I.

Mýrdalsjökull

Vestmannaeyjar

Vík

Surtsey I.

NORTH ATLANTIC OCEAN

Selected National Parks

① Fjallabak Reserve
② Jökulsárgljúfur NP
③ Skaftafell NP
④ Þingvellir NP

Out of Fire, Into Ice

Öræfajökull, a glacier in southeast Iceland

I CELAND IS A LIVING GEOLOGY LESSON. It is a land of active volcanoes, oozing lava, and jolting earthquakes. It also has sprawling glaciers, ice-carved fjords, and spouting geysers. This is a land of opposites, where steaming hot springs lie less than 100 miles (160 km) from the Arctic Circle and spewing volcanoes both destroy and build.

Earth science explains the opposites that make up Iceland. Sections of land called plates form the Earth's crust. When these plates meet, they create and destroy landmasses. One such meeting place is the Mid-Atlantic Ridge, an underwater mountain range roughly 10,800 miles (17,400 km) long beneath the Atlantic Ocean.

About 100 million years ago, the American and Eurasian plates forming the Mid-Atlantic Ridge began to separate. Magma (molten rock) from the Earth's liquid core seeped from a fissure, or crack, where the plates parted and built Iceland. This island nation forms an ever-widening saddle over the Mid-Atlantic Ridge. The plates continue to spread at a rate of 1 inch (2.5 centimeters) per year, and lava seals the opening.

While forces beneath the Earth's crust provide Iceland's fire, its near–North Atlantic location explains the ice. In the last Ice Age, glaciers blanketed the entire 39,756-square-mile

Opposite: **One of Iceland's one hundred volcanoes spews molten lava.**

Iceland's Geographical Features

Highest Elevation: Hvannadalshnúkur, 6,952 feet (2,119 m)

Lowest Elevation: Sea level along the coast

Longest River: Þjórsá, 144 miles (230 km)

Largest Glacier: Vatnajökull, 3,200 square miles (8,300 sq km)

Greatest Distance East to West: 300 miles (483 km)

Greatest Distance North to South: 190 miles (306 km)

Most Active Volcano: Mount Hekla, last eruption, 2000

Most Powerful Geyser: Strokkur, spouts about 100 feet (30 m)

Newest Island: Surtsey, formed 1963 by an active volcano

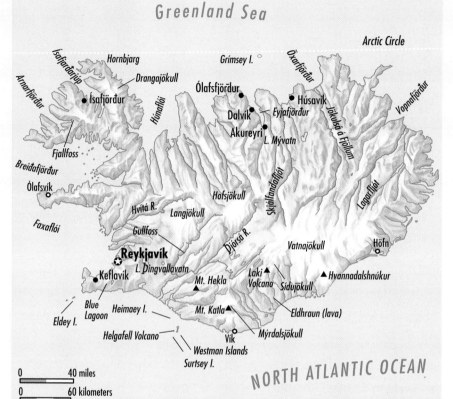

Largest Lake: Þingvallavatn, 32 square miles (83 sq km)

Largest Hot Spring: Deildartunguhver, yields 66 gallons (250 l) per second of nearly boiling water

(103,000-square-kilometer) island. Ice caps now cover about 10 percent of the island although scientific tests show today's glaciers were formed in more recent times.

From north to south, the island measures only 190 miles (306 km), so Iceland's southernmost tip—Surtsey Island—is a mere ninety-minute plane ride from the Arctic. On a world map, you'll find that Iceland's latitude is equal to that of Canada's Northwest Territories and the upper half of Russia.

From a Sea of Fire

Scientists believe that Iceland's volcanic activity created one-third of the lava produced on Earth in the past 500 years. Iceland has more than one hundred volcanoes although it is difficult to determine the exact number. Many lie hidden beneath massive ice caps or underwater along Iceland's coastline.

Mount Hekla in southwestern Iceland, called the "mouth of Hell," is the country's most active volcano. Hekla's fireworks lit the sky when the Vikings first settled Iceland, and the volcano still threatens the island today. Hekla's most recent eruption took place in 2000.

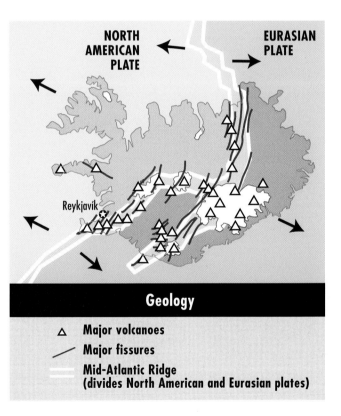

The country's most devastating volcanic event occurred in 1783 when southeastern Iceland's Laki spewed lava, poisonous gas, and ash over the land. Dust clouds damaged crops, and about 70 percent of the country's livestock died. As a result, food became scarce, and famine killed 20 percent of Iceland's population.

The Icelandic landscape often resembles the Moon's surface. Craters

Steam rises over the moon-like landscape of Iceland.

mark the land, forming lakes and basins. Steam clouds hang heavily over hot springs and geysers. Scalding volcanic mud pots bubble like gravy over an open flame.

Volcanic formations can be strange yet attractive. Near Lake Mývatn, the lava pillars of Dimmuborgir—some reaching 65 feet (20 meters) high—create a science fiction–like badlands. Eldhraun, a lifeless sprawl of lava rock found near Laki, is so similar to the Moon's surface that *Apollo 11* astronauts, the first men to walk on the Moon, trained for their moonwalks on Eldhraun's lava rock.

Volcanoes continue to build Iceland. The 1973 eruption on Heimaey, for example, increased the size of that island by about 15 percent. Even more dramatic, however, was the "birth" of Surtsey in 1963.

"Black castles" of lava rise above Lake Mývatn.

Quick! The Town Is On Fire!

On a dark January night in 1973, residents of Heimaey fled from their homes when gas, cinders, and hot lava spewed from a crack in the island's surface. All 5,300 islanders escaped to the mainland on ferries and fishing boats. For the next five months, lava oozed from the Earth, destroying 400 buildings, about one-third of the town.

A way to stop the oncoming lava had to be found. Icelandic geologist Thorbjörn Sigurgeirsson suggested spraying the lava with seawater. It worked! The nearly freezing water quickly cooled the molten lava from over 2000°Fahrenheit to 212°F

(1100°Celsius to 100°C). The cooled lava formed a crust and plugged the fissure, ending Heimaey's worst natural disaster.

Surtsey was formed by volcanic action beneath the sea.

In mid-November 1963, Icelandic fishermen noticed a volcanic eruption under the North Atlantic, about 12 miles (19.3 km) from Heimaey. Geologists and television crews quickly hired boats to take them to the site. To the delight of scientists and television viewers around the world, a new island literally burst from the sea. In just over three years, Surtsey grew into a full-size island.

Scientists have carefully monitored the changes on Surtsey since 1963. By 1987, twenty-five types of plants had grown on the island. Their seeds came to Surtsey by ocean currents, wind, or migrating birds. Today, five species of seabirds also make their homes on Surtsey, and seals sun themselves on the island's rugged beaches.

Along with volcanic activity comes a shifting and settling of the Earth, a geologic event called an earthquake. Icelanders feel tremors on a fairly regular basis. Most quakes cause little damage, but there is always the danger of "the big one."

Icelanders prepare for the tremors that rumble and grumble beneath them. At school, children practice earthquake drills. At home, household items such as plates, glassware, and food are carefully stored so that tremors do not damage them.

Carved by Ice

The land that was built by fire has also been carved by ice. For over 100,000 years, a thick sheet of ice covered Iceland. The weight and movement of the ice cap pressed down on the land below it. Where rock or soil was weak, glaciers gouged out riverbeds, ravines, valleys, and fjords. Over many thousands of

How Iceland Got Its Name

According to legend, Flóki Vilgerðarson and his family left Norway in their ship, intending to claim a homestead on the new land to the west. They arrived in the area now called the West Fjords during summertime, when the fishing was excellent, and the weather was mild. However, winter was not so kind. Most of Flóki's livestock starved to death and his family struggled to survive. By springtime, Flóki was ready to go home, but thick ice blocked the fjord. He called the land Ísland (pronounced "eesland"), or "ice land."

The fishing village of Hornafjördur sits upon glacier-carved land.

years, the great ice cap slowly melted, leaving behind a land sculpted by ice.

Iceland's current glaciers formed about 2,500 years ago during a period of cold, wet weather. Today, most of Iceland's glaciers are retreating—each year, more ice melts than forms. However, it will take thousands of years to melt Vatnajökull, Langjökull, Hofsjökull, and the dozens of other glaciers that crown Iceland's mountain peaks. Meltwater from the glaciers feeds many of Iceland's raging rivers.

Vatnajökull—the largest glacier in Europe—covers about 3,200 square miles (8,300 sq km). The ice cap covers an area the size of Delaware and Rhode Island combined. At its greatest depth, Vatnajökull's ice is more than 3,000 feet (900 m) thick. The ice cap absorbs all available water, leaving the surrounding region surprisingly dry. The dryness has reduced the area to almost desert-like conditions.

Glaciers cap several active volcanoes, and when these volcanoes erupt, the damage can be disastrous. For example, Mýrdalsjökull lies over Mount Katla Volcano. When Katla erupts, the lava melts the underside of the glacier, forming a massive pool of meltwater that can burst forth in a sudden flood, called a *hlaup*. One such hlaup released 261,600 cubic yards (200,000 cubic meters) of water per second—a wall of water and sediment with the power of a tidal wave.

Hikers explore the largest glacier in Europe, Vatnajökull.

The Land

Iceland stretches out in a large plateau with the island's center higher than the surrounding coastline. Virtually all of Iceland's mountain peaks are volcanic. The highest peak, Hvannadalshnúkur, rises to 6,952 feet (2,119 m) in southeastern Iceland. Central and southeastern Iceland are mostly unsuitable for settlers. A road crosses the region, but there are no towns.

Farms and towns lie along the coast where the soil supports plant life. Most farmers raise livestock and grow hay and potatoes. Because the Vikings were seafaring folk, towns blossomed around bays and natural harbors. Fishing, fish processing, and shipping have become major industries in Iceland's cities.

Water, Water, Water

Iceland's abundant water plays a role in business, home life, and recreation and contributes to Iceland's natural beauty. Underground hot springs provide heat and energy. Delicate waterfalls tumble into deep gorges, sending fountains of mist into the air. Narrow fjords form protective harbors for the country's fishing fleet, which challenges the harsh North Atlantic Ocean in search of the day's catch.

Magma lying near the Earth's surface heats underground water throughout Iceland. Geysers and hot springs release this hot water to the surface. Iceland's best-known geyser—Great Geysir—has been dormant for about thirty years. Almost directly north of Reykjavík, Deildartunguhver, Iceland's largest hot spring, yields 66 gallons (250 l) per second of nearly boiling water.

Hot water erupts with great force from this geyser.

Iceland's geothermal water heats swimming pools and even bakes rye bread. About 85 percent of Iceland's homes and businesses are heated with geothermal energy. In the future, Iceland hopes to harness steam from the hot springs and turn it into electricity.

Rivers and streams flow throughout the country. Iceland's longest river, the Þjórsá, runs 144 miles (230 km) from north-central Iceland to the North Atlantic Ocean in the southwest. Many rivers, filled with rocks and soil, flow from the glaciers. The soil turns the water of glacial rivers brownish in color. Clear-water rivers flow with runoff from rain and melting snow or are fed by underground springs. Besides the Þjórsá, Iceland's major rivers include the Hvítá River in the southwest, the Blanda River in the northwest, Skjálfandafljót in the north, and Lagarfljót in the east.

Hothouse Fruits and Vegetables

Iceland is known for its glaciers, snowstorms—and bananas. Yes, bananas, along with tomatoes, lettuce, and cucumbers grow throughout the year in Iceland's geothermally heated greenhouses.

Hvítá River

The Gullfoss

Tumbling rivers frequently feed Iceland's magnificent waterfalls. The Gullfoss on the Hvítá River pours over a steep cliff and crashes into the pool below. The stunning Fjallfoss spills over the edge of a mountain, plunging 328 feet (100 m) toward the Arnarfjörður. Below the Fjallfoss, smaller waterfalls create a scenic wonderland.

Iceland's many lakes are fairly small. Both volcanoes and glaciers have formed these lakes. Volcanic lakes, like Mývatn in the north, are usually water-filled craters. The country's largest lake, Þingvallavatn, measures 32 square miles (83 sq km) and lies directly east of Reykjavík. Glacial lakes formed when retreating ice carved basins in the land.

Deep fjords slice harbors into the sheer cliffs lining much of Iceland's coastline. The larger fjords, such as Ísafjarðardjúp in the west and Eyjafjörður in the north, serve as ports for most of the year, although ice floes sometimes appear in bay water. Narrower inlets freeze solid during winter months, blocking ship travel.

Regions of Iceland

No clear relationship exists between Iceland's regions and its geographic features. The regions aren't defined by mountain ranges, major rivers, or desert plains. For example, Vatnajökull lies in three different regions: the South, Northeast, and East.

South and West Iceland include Cape Reykjanes, extensive farmland, and most of Iceland's people. Lake Þingvallavatn, Þingvellir National Park, and Reykjavík are among the sights that draw tourists. Few visitors pass up an opportunity to soak in the Blue Lagoon, a stunningly beautiful hot spring not far from Reykjavík.

Bathers enjoy the warm geothermally heated waters of the Blue Lagoon.

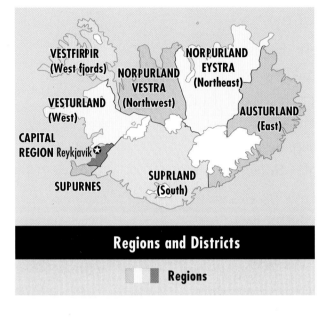

Regions and Districts

Regions

Vestmannaeyjar, or the Westman Islands, including Heimaey and Surtsey, stretch out from the southern coast. The islands mark an active volcanic region, which doesn't seem to bother seabirds, seals, or whales—just the people who live there. The Westman Islands are home to more than 10 million puffins!

"Wild," "rugged," and "dramatic" accurately describe the landscape of western Iceland above Reykjavík. Raging glacial rivers and lovely, lacey waterfalls cut through dense woodlands. Rocky islands dot the shoreline near Ólafsvík, where whale watching draws tourists and Icelanders alike.

The West Fjords, to the northwest, are Europe's western-most point. After the barren, uninhabited central region, the West Fjords have the lowest population. Its towns are small and isolated, particularly when winter ice cuts off ship travel.

Akureyri is the central city of the north. Like much of Iceland, the scenery in this region is starkly beautiful. Near Lake Mývatn, for example, geothermal activity combines with surface minerals to literally paint the fields in a rainbow of colors. Dettifoss, Europe's most powerful waterfall, is a must-see for tourists who are willing to trek to Iceland's far north.

The eastern region is surprising in that the land is mostly rolling hills, covered with emerald-green fields and valleys.

Sheep graze among the rounded hills in eastern Iceland.

Sheep and dairy farms occupy much of eastern Iceland. This area is also home to wild Icelandic horses and herds of reindeer.

A Look at Icelandic Cities

Akureyri (population 15,635) is Iceland's second-largest city (pictured). Although it is only 60 miles (100 km) from the Arctic Circle, it has surprisingly warm summer weather with temperatures reaching 68°F (20°C). Akureyri means "meadow sand-spit"—an appropriate name because it lies at the sandy end of Eyjafjörður Harbor. The Akureyri Folk Museum offers a visual record of the region since the early 1800s. Many of Akureyri's citizens trawl, can, and freeze fish at Iceland's largest fishery, the Akureyri Fishing Company.

Ísafjörður (population 2,741) in northwest Iceland is the commercial center of the West Fjords. The town is surrounded by water on three sides and backs up against sheer rock cliffs. Fishing is the primary industry in Ísafjörður. The town's West Fjords Maritime Museum gives visitors a glimpse of Iceland's long seafaring history.

Loud arguments erupt whenever Icelanders talk about Keflavík (population 7,930). This town in southwestern Iceland features a North Atlantic Treaty Organization (NATO) air base that has more than 5,000 U.S. servicemen. Even though 850 Icelanders work on the base, most Icelanders do not like having a NATO military presence in their country.

Out of Fire, Into Ice **29**

Aurora Borealis

One of the most delightful spectacles in Iceland is free. The aurora borealis is a dazzling phenomenon during which particles high above the night sky glow green, red, and purple. These streams of light bend and sway, dance and stretch. Auroras occur most frequently near the Earth's poles, which makes Iceland the ideal spot for nature's laser light show.

Nights of Sunshine, Days of Darkness

During Iceland's summers, the sun barely sets below the horizon. Likewise, on some winter days, the sun barely shines at all. On Grímsey off the north coast, the sun never dips below the sea on June 21, the longest day of the year. Farther south, in Reykjavík, daylight lasts about 21 hours on June 21.

Icelandic winter days are bleak, with many days of pale twilight replacing sunshine. On December 21, the shortest day of the year, sunrise and sunset are a brief four hours apart in Reykjavík. Grímsey sees even less sun on the winter solstice—barely two or three hours.

A Surprisingly Temperate Climate

Considering Iceland's near-Arctic location, you might expect to wear a parka and snow boots in mid-July. However, Iceland's climate is actually quite mild. The Gulf Stream, a current of warm water that travels up the Atlantic from the Gulf of Mexico, heats up the island. That's not to say that Icelandic summers are tropical—Reykjavík's average July temperature is a brisk 52°F (11°C). Even winter temperatures rarely drop below 0°F (–18°C) in Reykjavík.

Weather is both a concern and a passion with Icelanders. Bitter cold, snow, and freezing winds come to Iceland from Greenland to the west while warm breezes, rain, and mild temperatures ride along the Gulf Stream. The two weather patterns clash in an ever-changing, ever-challenging climate.

This Icelander battles fierce winds during a storm.

The one certain thing about Icelandic weather is that there will be wind. When chilling Arctic gusts bluster, Icelanders like to point out that it's never the temperature that's the problem—it's the wind. The strongest winds whip through the Westman Islands. In 1973 and again in 1991, winds gusted to 165 miles (264 km) per hour—the highest measurable reading on wind instruments.

Puffins, Horses, and Moss

THE STARK, SPARE LAND OF ICELAND HAS AN UNCOMMON beauty with its sheer cliffs, deep fjords, and barren deserts. Yet this curious land bursts with wildlife and blooms with plants.

Opposite: **An Icelandic horse stands near the Hvítá River.**

Beneath the Sea

Great schools of cod, herring, redfish, and capelin thrive in the bitter-cold North Atlantic seas off Iceland's shores. These fish are the main catch for Iceland's fishing fleet. However, they are only a small portion of the vast community of creatures living in Iceland's seas.

Huge pink-fleshed Atlantic salmon and slithering sea eels migrate to Iceland's waters every year. Shrimp, lobster, and

Lobsters are in abundance along the North Atlantic seabed.

A harbor seal lounges in the frigid Icelandic water.

clams hug the rocky seafloor near the island, while rugged lava rock provides an anchor for barnacles, urchins, and mussels at the water's edge.

Swarms of krill—small shrimp-like creatures—churn up the seas, feeding minke and humpback whales. Seventeen species of whales swim in Iceland's frigid waters. On a lucky day, a keen watcher might spot sperm, fin, or bowhead whales.

Harbor seals and gray seals jockey for space on remote coastal islands or black-sand fjord beaches. Seals set up their nurseries on Iceland's shores, and about half the world's population of harbor seals live on or near Iceland.

Living Beside the Sea

Millions of seabirds nest on the ledges of Iceland's sheer cliffs. Each spring brings a flurry of wings as birds of the northern seas, such as murres, puffins, fulmars, guillemots, and gannets, build nests and lay eggs above the icy waters.

The bright-beaked, parrot-like puffin is extremely popular with Icelanders. Nesting pairs build burrows for their chicks on sea cliffs. By late summer, puffin parents give up feeding their ever-hungry chicks, and the young are forced to fend for themselves. Many find their way to the village on Heimaey, where children put them in boxes to protect them from local cats and dogs. The chicks are then cast out to sea the following day, hopefully to begin a successful journey to adulthood.

Sea cliffs are a good resting place for these puffins.

The Last Great Auk

The great auk, the largest member of the auk family, had one major disadvantage—it could not fly. These large black-and-white birds nested on small rocky islands called skerries. Their exposed nests made it easy to hunt the birds and collect their eggs. Excessive hunting and a volcanic eruption all but wiped out the species. Then, in 1844, museum collectors killed the last great auks on Eldey Island. The great auk is now extinct.

Farmers welcome the sight of ravens that keep rodents away from their fields.

Birds of Prey

The abundant sea, lakes, and bird life in Iceland provide ample food for many birds of prey. The island is home to the common raven as well as the less ordinary eagle, falcon, and merlin.

Icelandic farmers offer a warm welcome to nesting ravens. Traditionally, the raven holds an important place in Norse mythology, though modern-day farmers accept nesting ravens mainly because they keep the mouse population under control.

The largest Icelandic bird of prey, with a wingspan of about 8 feet (2.5 m), is the white-tailed eagle—a relative of the bald eagle. In the

1800s, many farmers believed white-tailed eagles carried away newborn lambs and the eggs and chicks of eider ducks. To protect their livestock, the farmers tried to kill all of Iceland's eagles.

The white-tailed eagle soon became endangered through overhunting and poisoning. By 1920, only ten nesting pairs of white-tailed eagles still lived in Iceland. The population has since increased to forty pairs but is still in danger of extinction.

High above Iceland's cliffs, the noble gyrfalcons search for their next meals. The gyrfalcon averages 2 feet (61 centimeters) in length, and its wingspan stretches 4 to 5 feet (1.2 to 1.5 m). Its large, powerful body and sharp beak make the gyrfalcon a great hunter. These majestic birds prey on gulls, snow geese, ptarmigans, grouse, and ducks—all abundant throughout Iceland.

Traditionally, Icelanders prized gyrfalcons as a valued resource and sold them to the highest bidder. During the Middle Ages (from A.D. 500 to 1500), European falconers and nobles imported gyrfalcons for hunting. Today the birds are protected by law, but some poachers still net and sell gyrfalcons to wealthy collectors. An adult gyrfalcon sells for as much as $100,000.

Bird-watchers find merlins throughout Iceland's open hills and wetlands. Merlins hunt in the daytime, looking for small birds, insects, and mice. Iceland's merlins survive mostly on songbirds, such as redwings and wheatears. In Iceland, there are more merlins than any other bird of prey.

Waterfowl and Songbirds

Iceland's marshes and wetlands are popular nesting spots for waterfowl and wading birds. In the summer, these birds migrate to Iceland, where food is plentiful and people are few.

Graceful whooper swans glide on smooth Icelandic lakes, while golden plovers wade along the shoreline in search of fish. Early in spring, thousands of greylag geese, pink-footed geese, and ducks build nests in tall marsh grasses. Their goslings and ducklings must be ready to fly south before the fierce Icelandic winter begins.

A mother whooper swan followed by her young

Songbirds also flock to Iceland. Redwings, wrens, and starlings find plentiful berries and plant buds but few trees in which to build nests. Wheatears and meadow pipits dine on Iceland's swarming insects.

Animals on the Land

When settlers first arrived in Iceland, they found only one mammal—the arctic fox. These sly hunters are described as either blue or white. Although most arctic foxes are pictured with thick, snow-colored fur, only one-third of Iceland's arctic foxes are white.

Early settlers brought "stowaways" with them on their ships—rats and mice. Today, four types of rodents live in Iceland, including long-tailed field mice, house mice, brown rats, and black rats. Rats and house mice can be found in Iceland's towns and cities. Field mice thrive on wild berries, moss, wild mushrooms, and some farm crops.

Icelanders have imported a number of animals for agricultural or economic reasons. Humans owe their survival on the island to farm animals, such as sheep, cattle, and poultry. Icelandic horses, first introduced to the island more than 1,000 years ago, furnished transportation for hundreds of years.

Not every imported animal proved profitable for Icelanders, though. Their least successful attempts were reindeer herding and mink farming.

An Accidental Tourist

On rare occasions, polar bears find themselves on Iceland's shores. During winter months, ice floes and ice sheets stretch from Greenland to Iceland. A wandering bear might drift eastward on a floe or even walk from one island to the other. Iceland, although teeming with food for a hungry polar bear, is actually too warm for these arctic dwellers.

The Icelandic Horse

Rugged, shaggy, and sturdy, the Icelandic horse has been a key element in sheep farming for centuries. The Vikings introduced this breed to Iceland, and it was the sole source of transportation there until the 1800s.

To protect these strong animals, the Icelandic government does not allow horses to be imported into the country. This law protects Iceland's horses from diseases, such as foot-and-mouth disease.

Reindeer hunt for food beneath the winter snow.

Between 1771 and 1787, dozens of reindeer were brought to Iceland from Norway, and some Icelanders were supposed to become reindeer herders. Neither the herders nor the reindeer cooperated, however. The herd returned to the wild. By 1817, the wild reindeer population had grown to a point where their grazing threatened to damage open pastures. Reindeer were hunted without government control, and the herd size soon dropped to almost nothing. A ban on reindeer hunting from 1901 through 1940 allowed the herd to multiply, and the current reindeer herd now numbers about 3,000.

In the early 1930s, fur farming became popular in Iceland. Hopeful fur farmers introduced mink to the island. Unfortunately, the experiment was a disaster. A number of mink escaped and found Iceland's wet, rugged wilderness to their liking. Mink are quick breeders and eager hunters who have no natural enemies in Iceland. As a result, their population has grown rapidly throughout the country. While some mink farmers are starting to show a profit from their efforts, the wild mink population problem continues with no solution in sight.

Hardy Plants Wanted

Birch forests covered much of the land when the first settlers arrived in Iceland. The Vikings immediately cut down these forests for wood for building and fuel and to clear land for farming. The Vikings did not realize that Iceland's thin layer of soil could not support large grain fields or heavy livestock grazing. By the end of the Settlement Age in A.D. 930, sixty years of cutting had reduced the forests to about 5 percent of the original wooded area. Erosion and grazing wiped out fields of moss and native herbs. Today, less than 1 percent of the original forests remain.

About 470 flowering plant species are native to Iceland. They include sea plants and grasses, trees and shrubs, and an array of wildflowers. Most native plants found on Iceland can also be found in Norway, Northern Ireland, and Scotland.

Though not appetizing looking, kelp provides vitamins and minerals to an Icelandic diet.

Kelp, wrack, and dulse are sea vegetables found along Iceland's coast. Although they may not look appetizing, some sea plants are both edible and nutritious. Dark red dulse, brown knotted wrack, and bladder wrack cling to coastal rocks. As food, dulse provides the daily requirement of vitamin B_6, as well as vitamin B_{12}, iron, and potassium. Just offshore, dark green kelp beds sway with the tides. Dried kelp, sold in health-food stores, is an excellent source of calcium, iodine, zinc, and B vitamins.

Along the shores and in marshes and wetlands, grasses and bulrushes grow in thick clusters. Eelgrass and sea-meadow grass shelter nesting waterbirds and slow wind and water erosion. Along the water's edge, crabs, clams, and small fish use eelgrass as a nursery for their young.

The few trees that thrive in Iceland are low-lying birches and willows. Strong winds and thin topsoil keep tree growth to a minimum. Blueberry, bearberry, and crowberry shrubs grow wild throughout most of Iceland, however, and their berries make excellent eating.

Wetland wildflowers sprinkle color amid reeds and grasses. Delicate clusters of pink sea rocket, vivid yellow

Buttercups splash yellow on an Icelandic coastal meadow.

Moss, common to Iceland, thrives in lava fields.

silverweed, and brilliant blue harebell paint Iceland's marshes. At higher elevations, Iceland poppies wave orange and yellow against the green-gray moss and lichens of the rugged highlands.

By far, the most common native plants in Iceland are moss and lichens, which grow easily in shallow soil or on barren lava fields. In all, Iceland boasts more than 500 types of moss, 450 types of lichens, and about 250 types of fungi (mushrooms). Their spongy, dense growth survives heavy rainfall, long winters, and icy winds.

Making the Most of Moss

Most people do not think of moss as an important part of their diets. Icelanders, however, eat moss in a variety of ways. It can be served as a sauce with milk, used as a sausage ingredient, or boiled in milk as porridge.

Wind and water erosion need constant attention. The little topsoil that exists in Iceland is thin and easily damaged. Volcanic eruptions, earthquakes, and glacial floods also do their share of harm. Handling Iceland's natural resources is the responsibility of the Soil Conservation Service and the Forestry Service. Both agencies were established in 1907, but real concern over protecting the environment came only after the nation's independence in 1944. Iceland's first major environmental law was the Nature Conservation Act of 1956, which established the country's first national parks and preserves.

A new government department, the Ministry for the Environment, was formed in 1990. This department oversees national parks and preserves, protects endangered species, and deals with issues concerning pollution. Today, Iceland has eighty-two nature preserves and four national parks. A new park planned for 2002 at Vatnajökull will be Europe's largest national park.

The country's most historic national park is Þingvellir, site of the first Alþing. Þingvellir, or "Parliament Plains," has both historic and natural importance for Icelanders. The park lies along Iceland's largest lake, Þingvallavatn. Summertime wildflowers and autumn leaves paint the plains with yellows, purples, and reds.

In contrast, Skaftafell National Park, founded in 1956, sprawls high among Iceland's largest glaciers. Skaftafell has a dramatic, harsh beauty that is hard to describe. Surrounding the park are startling white glaciers, deep blue lakes, and untamed mountains. Among the strange sights of Skaftafell are tunnels through dense ice and frozen waterfalls.

During the summer months, people flock to Skaftafell to get a close view of Vatnajökull on the park's southern edge. Many visitors enjoy hiking on the sweeping moors that lie between the high mountain peaks.

Tourists stroll the Almannagja fissure in Þingvellir.

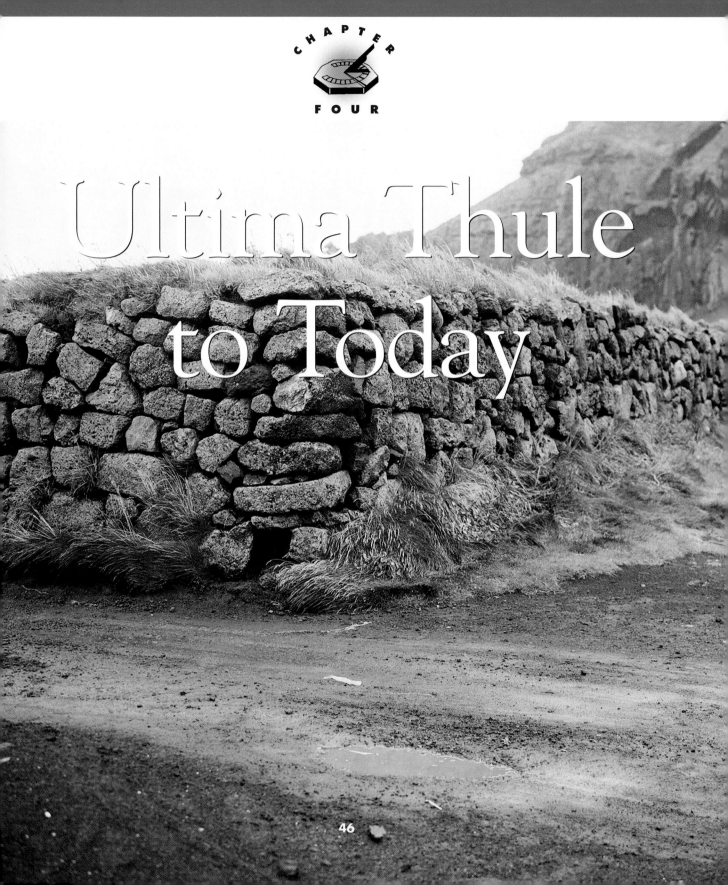

Ultima Thule to Today

U NLIKE MOST COUNTRIES, ICELAND'S COMPLETE HISTORY is recorded. No prehistoric tribes, cave dwellers, or hunter-gatherer clans lived there. Iceland had no ancient civilizations because no humans lived permanently on the island until A.D. 874.

The first documented mention of the island comes from material written by the Greek explorer Pytheas. Pytheas traveled from France in 330 B.C. and sailed beyond the British Isles, sighting a previously unknown island that some historians believe was Iceland. According to Pytheas's log, the island was a six-day sail from Britain. Pytheas called the newly discovered land *ultima thule,* or "the end of the world."

More than 1,100 years passed before Iceland appeared once again in written records. In A.D. 825, an Irish monk named Dicuil wrote a geography book called *De Mensura Orbis Terrae* (*The Description of the Earth's Sphere*). Dicuil described an island northwest of Ireland that served for many years as a summer vacation spot for Irish priests. Again, historians think this was Iceland.

Opposite: **Ruins of the seventeenth-century Fort Skanzin on Heimaey**

A map of thule, first described by Pytheas

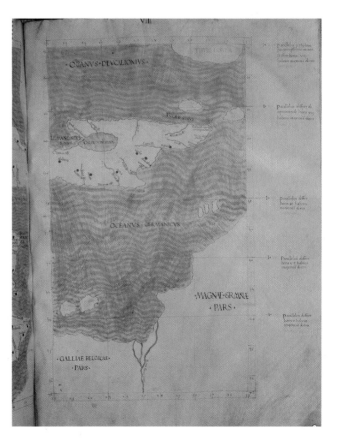

The Book of Settlements

Until the Vikings arrived in A.D. 874, no permanent settlements were established in Iceland or on its neighboring islands. Prior to Iceland's settlement, Norway's King Harald the Fairhaired and other powerful Norwegian lords had argued over land rights. Harald had won and had forced the losers to leave Norway. Some had gone to Scotland; others had headed farther west to the country we now call Iceland.

Information about the Settlement Age (A.D. 874–930) comes mainly from the twelfth-century *Landnámabók* (*Book of Settlements*). This book provides a fairly accurate census of the 400 Viking settlers who lived in Iceland at that time. According to the book, Ingólfur Arnarson was the first Viking to build a home and settle his family there.

Very little land was worth farming, and early settlers quickly claimed the best land. However, most scraped out a meager living from the poor volcanic soil. They supplemented their food supply with salmon and trout from the rivers and fish from the sea.

Families built longhouses in which they lived along with relatives, followers, and servants. In Iceland, usually only the frame of a house was made of wood. Stone walls formed the foundation, and blocks of

A family, its relatives, and others lived in these wood, stone, and moss homes.

turf (soil plus grass or moss) were used to make walls and a roof. An open fire, used for heating and cooking, burned in the center of the house. Livestock lived inside the house with the family during the long, cold winter months.

The Saga Age

In 930, many settlers met at Þingvellir and formed a government, the Alþing. This government was unique at that time because it was run by elected leaders, set up laws for all Icelandic citizens, and formed a court to try people who broke those laws. No single person in Iceland was all-powerful—the Icelanders had endured enough from Norway's king and didn't want to repeat the experience.

Keeping track of laws passed by the Alþing became the job of the Law Speaker. This elected official memorized the laws and recited one-third of them at the Alþing annual meeting. When the Law Speaker spoke, he stood on the Law Rock above all who were present. This site is preserved today as part of Iceland's heritage.

The Saga Age, a time of heroic feats, daring crimes, and noble leaders, followed settlement. From the ninth century through the early twelfth century, *skalds* (poets) and law speakers memorized Iceland's historic records and kept them alive. The country's many laws remained unwritten until 1119. The people relied on the memories of dozens of law speakers to accurately recall all their laws.

By the end of the Settlement Age, all of Iceland's fertile land had been claimed. Anyone who wanted to own land had to find

Eirík the Red

it elsewhere. Late in the tenth century, Icelander Eirík the Red set out with twenty-five ships loaded with settlers. They headed west and found the island we now call Greenland.

The people formed two new colonies: Eystri Byggð (Eastern Settlement) and Vesturbyggð (Western Settlement). Farming and fishing provided food. The settlers also hunted seals for their skins and meat and melted the blubber for oil. It was from Greenland that Leif Eiríksson, Eirík the Red's son, traveled westward to the North American continent. Although they were the first Europeans in North America, Leif and his people never built a permanent settlement.

Leif the Lucky

No one is sure how Leif Eiríksson (about 970–1020) came to discover North America, which he called Vínland. How he actually got there is still questioned.

The most believable story claims that Leif heard about land sighted by his friend, Bjarni Herjúlfsson. Interested in seeing the new land, Leif bought Bjarni's boat and sailed westward. The second story places Leif on a trip to Greenland, ordered by King Olaf of Norway to convert the Greenlanders to Christianity. Leif missed Greenland, however, and landed in North America. Either way, Leif landed on the continent about 500 years before Columbus arrived.

It was in A.D. 1000 that Iceland's government chose to adopt Christianity. While some countries battled over religion, Iceland's leaders took the same approach toward Christianity as they did toward most other changes—they took a vote. The proposal for accepting Christianity was approved. No other country can claim such a peaceful, organized change of religion.

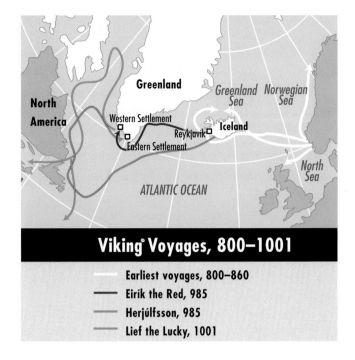

Viking Voyages, 800–1001

- Earliest voyages, 800–860
- Eirík the Red, 985
- Herjúlfsson, 985
- Lief the Lucky, 1001

Golden Age Gives Way to Violence

The exploits of Iceland's Vikings inspired a Golden Age of Literature—the Age of Writing (1120–1230). The popular

Illustration from a fourteenth-century collection of Icelandic sagas

form for storytelling was the saga—a prose epic. Sagas told of early settlers, great outlaws, and feats of daring and skill. The Viking language of the sagas is the same language spoken in Iceland today. These prose narratives are stored in Iceland's National Archives, and their original texts are read easily by Icelandic-speaking visitors.

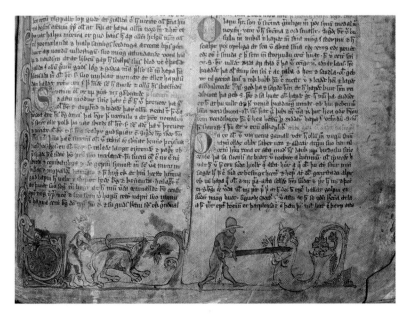

An Icelandic Storyteller

Snorri Sturluson (1179–1241) is considered the greatest of Iceland's storytellers. He told stories from Iceland's past that are still admired today. Some historians believe Snorri wrote the *Snorra Edda* and possibly *Egils Saga*.

Snorri gained wealth and power through his marriage to the heiress of Borg. A respected chieftain, Snorri was appointed Law Speaker in 1215 and again in 1222. Snorri was often described as greedy and ambitious.

The details of Snorri's death are clear: he was murdered. He dealt dishonestly with Norway's King Hákon, who sent a man to kill Snorri. The murder was carried out on September 22, 1241.

The Golden Age of Literature dwindled away during the early part of the thirteenth century. There were fewer chieftains and of course fewer clans. Among the remaining powerful clans were Hvamm-Sturla's relatives. The Sturlung Age (1230–1264), literally the era of Sturla's children, brought Iceland's Golden Age to an end. Political backstabbing, violence, and bloody battles replaced 200 years of peace and freedom.

To stop the lawlessness and the fighting, the Alþing asked Norway's king Hákon to bring law and order to the land. In return for his help, the Icelandic government passed a law giving the king power to tax Icelanders. King Hákon saw an opportunity to add to his power and took it. In 1262, Iceland lost its independence and became a colony of Norway.

Colonial Rule

The 1300s were a time of natural disasters, plagues, and hunger for many Icelanders. Mount Hekla erupted in 1300, 1341, and again in 1381. These eruptions killed livestock, destroyed crops, and left Iceland's farmers in a desperate situation. Each major eruption was followed by a severe winter with heavy snowfalls. The following springs brought destructive flooding.

For Iceland, this period was particularly harsh. Although Icelanders had products to sell and a desire to buy, the Norwegian king prohibited Iceland from trading with other countries. Norway wanted to get rich by selling Iceland's fish but never kept to a regular shipping schedule.

Norway, too, had its share of woes. In the 1300s, trade between European nations was common. This open, active trading brought more than merchandise to Norway; it also brought the bubonic plague, or Black Death. As Norway fought the plague, Iceland—dependent on food and supplies from Norway—struggled to survive.

Black Death

Between 1334 and 1351, an epidemic of bubonic plague, or Black Death, spread across Asia and Europe, killing millions of people. A germ carried by rats caused the plague. It was transmitted by fleas, which bit infected rats then humans.

The plague wiped out nearly one-fourth of Europe's population. From 1402–1404, another bubonic plague struck Iceland, killing many people.

In 1380, something startling happened in Norway. The royal family died out! Norway and its holdings, including Iceland, then fell under the control of Denmark's king Ólaf, an infant. His mother, Queen Margrete, served as leader in his place. Denmark followed Norway's policies toward Iceland, largely ignoring the colony.

When pirates raided coastal villages, which happened frequently, the Danish government showed no interest in Iceland. On the other hand, Denmark forcibly limited trade so that Iceland could not replace needed supplies. Denmark bought Iceland's fish at low prices and sold Icelanders much-needed finished goods and food at great cost. Then, the Black Death struck Iceland in the early 1400s, all but destroying the country's population.

It didn't seem possible, but Iceland's situation got worse. Under Danish rule, Icelanders lost freedoms that were considered rights under Icelandic law. In the 1500s, the Reformation, a religious revolt against the Roman Catholic Church, began in Europe. Denmark accepted the teachings of Martin Luther and Lutheranism, and Iceland was forced to follow Denmark's lead.

Kingdom of Norway, Early 1300s

Kingdom of Norway

This religious change was not nearly as peaceful as the acceptance of Christianity had been in 1000. In 1526, Lutheran bishop Ögmund of Skálholt and Roman Catholic bishop Jón Arason argued at the annual meeting of the Alþing and ended up dueling over the disagreement. More than twenty years later, anger between the churches still raged, as Bishop Jón led a rebellion against the Lutherans. The dispute finally ended in 1550, when Denmark's king Christian III had Bishop Jón beheaded. Lutheranism has been Iceland's national religion since then.

Greater Control by Denmark

In 1602, Denmark reduced economic opportunities for Iceland by limiting trade only to merchants licensed by the Danish king. The prices these merchants charged were outrageous. Imported products, such as flour, furniture, and metal goods, cost five times as much as they had before licensing began. At the same time, Icelandic fish brought in barely 20 percent of the money it should have.

Other European countries also saw Iceland as a prime target. In 1614, 3,000 British pirates swarmed over the Westman Islands, killing many Icelanders and taking others prisoner. The worst raid took place in 1627, when Algerian pirates made an assault on Iceland. The pirates arrived in five ships, attacking villages along the east coast. About 380 Icelanders were kidnapped and sold as slaves.

While Danish rules hurt Iceland's trade economy, natural disasters plagued the country's farms and towns. Erupting volcanoes and powerful earthquakes struck Iceland at least six times during the 1600s. Loss of livestock, farm crops, and property never seemed to end in troubled Iceland.

Icelanders welcomed the eighteenth century, hoping to see an end to the country's woes. They were disappointed. A census taken in 1703 showed Iceland's population to be about 50,000 people. By 1709, 15,000 of those 50,000 had died in a devastating smallpox epidemic.

Then, in 1783, the country suffered its worst volcanic eruption when the Laki Volcano flung ash, poisonous gas, and lava across the land. Iceland's situation was serious. Denmark's king finally changed trade rules so that all Danish subjects had the right to trade in Iceland. Although trading became easier, the impact of the eruption was too great. More than 11,400 head of cattle, 190,000 sheep, and 28,000 horses had died. Crop damage throughout the country was also severe. Iceland fell into a period of unrelieved famine, and outbreaks of smallpox added to the disaster. In all, one-third of Iceland's population died of hunger or disease.

Entering the Nineteenth Century

The nineteenth century opened with a major political change for Iceland. The Danish king stopped meetings of the Alþing in 1800. Icelanders could no longer elect officials to run their government. Instead, the Danish king appointed representatives, many of whom had trade interests in Iceland.

By 1843, the Danish government decided to reestablish the Alþing. The Icelandic representatives could only advise the Danes—not run Iceland. The new Alþing consisted of twenty Icelandic representatives and a handful of officials chosen by Denmark's king Christian VIII. Instead of meeting at Þingvellir, the new Alþing would meet in Reykjavík, which would serve as Iceland's capital. Trade policies now allowed Iceland free trade with any country, and political control eased.

Changes took place in Denmark as well. In 1849, Danish king Frederick VII approved major political, social, and economic changes, including the adoption of the country's first democratic constitution. Jón Sigurðsson proposed that Iceland be given independence at this time. His idea was rejected, but Sigurðsson refused to give up.

Jón Sigurðsson

Born in the West Fjords, Jón Sigurðsson (1811–1879) was raised with a passionate interest in Iceland and its heritage. Although he lived most of his adult life in Copenhagen, Denmark, Sigurðsson determined to lead his native Iceland to independence from Danish rule. Sigurðsson explained Iceland's viewpoint to Denmark's king. He claimed that Iceland had been forced to accept Denmark's rule, despite Icelanders' opposition to the idea. Freedom for Iceland came in small steps: home rule first, then sovereignty, and finally, independence. Iceland officially gained independence on July 17, 1944—the anniversary of Jón Sigurðsson's birthday.

In 1874, Iceland celebrated its one-thousandth-year anniversary since settlement. Denmark's king visited the country for the first time. A new constitution was approved and eventually led to home rule and independence.

Twentieth-Century Iceland

The early years of the twentieth century brought about significant political changes in Iceland. In 1904, Denmark gave

Hafstein and the Telephone

In the early 1900s, poet-politician Hannes Hafstein founded the Home Rule Party, a political group that wanted Iceland's leaders to actually live in Iceland instead of Denmark. Hafstein became the first minister when Iceland received home rule in 1904.

Hafstein believed that Iceland's economic survival depended on communication with the rest of the world. He suggested that cable be run to bring international telephone service to the country. Surprisingly, many Icelanders protested Hafstein's idea. They preferred to be separate from Europe. Still, the first international telephone service to Iceland began in 1906.

Icelanders the right to rule themselves. Political parties promoting almost every viewpoint sprang up. Politics in Iceland became as rough-and-tumble as a five-way tug-of-war.

Among the political issues under discussion were women's voting rights, Iceland's relationship with Denmark, and whether to allow the sale of alcoholic beverages. Prohibition, the law that made selling alcoholic drinks illegal, passed in 1909 although the law was unpopular. Iceland granted women the right to vote in national elections in 1917—three years before women in the United States got the right to vote. However, it was not until the end of World War I in 1918 that Iceland became a sovereign nation with its own national flag. At this point, Iceland was still considered part of Denmark.

For the next thirty years, Iceland fought to expand its economy. Fishing and fish processing became the leading industries. However, successful fishing depended on good weather, the strength of the competition, and the international market. Bad weather caused several poor fishing seasons and hurt the growing industry. Competition from other fishing nations increased, taking away part of Iceland's international market.

As the financial problems of the Great Depression (1929–1939) spread worldwide, less money was available to buy Icelandic fish. Sales decreased as the financial depression continued. Iceland, like many other countries, suffered high rates of unemployment and poverty. It took a world war to turn the struggling economy around.

Although Iceland avoided being drawn into World War I, the country could not escape World War II. In 1939, Germany invaded Poland and World War II (1939–1945) began. Germany, Austria-Hungary, Italy, and Japan were the major Axis countries. Great Britain, France, Russia, and eventually, the United States were the major countries making up the Allied forces.

By 1940, when Denmark and Iceland had planned to discuss independence, Germany had already invaded Denmark. Iceland had no chance to discuss independence so the Alþing took over complete rule of the country.

Icelanders hoped to remain neutral during the war, but Great Britain had a different idea. Britain recognized that Iceland's location was important to the war effort. The island could control shipping in the North Atlantic and serve as a supply depot for Allied ships.

U.S. soldiers transport a soldier with a mock injury during a practice air raid in Iceland.

Without any concern for Iceland's viewpoint, the British decided to capture Iceland before Germany could do so. Great Britain established a British post in Iceland with Operation Fork in Reykjavík. As a military operation, Operation Fork was poorly planned, undermanned, and undersupplied, but it was successful. On May 10, 1940, the British took over, and Iceland became a supply post for the Allies. A year later, Iceland and the United States signed a treaty that replaced British soldiers with Americans.

A Declaration of Freedom

In 1944, the Alþing issued the following resolution concerning their relationship to Denmark:

> The Alþing resolves to declare that it considers Iceland to have acquired the right to a complete breaking off of the union with Denmark, since it has now had to take into its own hand the conduct of all its affairs.

Freedom Amid War

As the war raged on, Iceland achieved a goal that had taken almost 100 years to reach. In April 1944, the Alþing approved the end of Iceland's relationship with Denmark. The country's voters were asked to agree to the move in a national vote. In all, 97 percent of Iceland's voters chose to declare independence. The victory was announced first over the radio, then by ringing church bells in every city and town.

On June 17, 1944, Iceland was once again a free and independent country. At historic Þingvellir, 20,000 Icelanders met to celebrate their return to full democracy. Sveinn Björnsson was elected Iceland's first president.

Iceland took its position in world politics seriously. In 1946, the country joined the newly formed United Nations. Three years later, it joined the North Atlantic Treaty Organization (NATO), but new problems arose. NATO wanted to put a permanent air base at Keflavík on Iceland's

Soldiers stand at attention at the Keflavík air base during the mid-1940s.

western shore. The Keflavík air base is still in use and continues to irritate Icelanders, who believe in their country's position of neutrality.

Fishing rights and practices have also been a source of trouble for Iceland. In 1975, Iceland officially expanded offshore limits to 200 nautical miles (320 km). The next year, Iceland entered into a "Cod War"—a dispute with Great Britain over Iceland's offshore fishing boundary. Similar arguments over fish quotas have arisen recently among Iceland and Norway, Russia, and the European Economic Union. Because fishing is Iceland's primary industry, the government does not feel it can give way on international fishing arguments.

Iceland Today

The 1980s saw dramatic achievements in Iceland. Vigdís Finnbogadóttir became the first woman ever elected as president of a republic. She held the office through four terms. Iceland also hosted an international summit meeting in 1986, where United States president Ronald Reagan and Soviet premier Mikhail Gorbachev discussed world affairs.

In the past, Iceland actively pursued commercial whaling, despite active protests by environmental groups. In 1992, the International Whaling Commission asked cooperating nations to support whaling quotas. Iceland refused, but Icelandic whalers have not resumed active whaling.

Iceland's economy has progressed, providing a stable financial base for its citizens. In 1995, Iceland ranked among the top twenty nations in the world in per-person income.

Today, it draws tourists and business from throughout the world. While tourism and industry bring needed money, the exposure to world problems has taken a toll on Iceland's quiet, peaceful existence. The country's first bank robbery took place in 1995. Human immunodeficiency virus (HIV) and acquired immunodeficiency syndrome (AIDS) have reached the island, and illegal drug use increases every year.

Natural disasters continue to plague Iceland too. In 1995, avalanches twice struck fishing villages in the West Fjords. Property damage was high, and thirty-four people died. In 1996 and again in 2001, floods from Vatnajökull swept across southeastern Iceland. The forces of nature that formed the island millions of years ago still play a role in the daily lives of Icelanders.

Alþing:
The Law of
Iceland

More than 1,000 years ago, Iceland's Law Speaker stood upon the Law Rock at Þingvellir. The gathered chieftains and their men grew silent as the Law Speaker began reciting the laws to the crowd.

At the Alþing, laws were passed and crimes were judged. The Alþing was the first parliament, and Iceland was a republic. This democracy thrived more than 800 years before the United States was even an idea.

Opposite: **Parliament building**

Iceland's Constitution

Iceland's constitution sets forth the rights and freedoms of Icelanders and the responsibilities of government toward the people. Icelanders adopted their constitution on the day the country declared independence from Denmark—June 17, 1944.

Many Icelandic rights are similar to the rights of U.S. citizens. Icelanders are free to follow their chosen religions, although the constitution names the Church of Iceland as the state church. Citizens accused of breaking laws must receive a speedy court trial, and the police need a search warrant to look through a person's home or property.

One constitutional right that is taken very seriously is the right to vote. All Icelanders over age eighteen can vote.

Icelanders turn out to vote for members of Parliament.

More than 200,000 Icelanders are of voting age. At each election the voting rate is about 85 percent. Politicians actively compete in elections. Their campaigns are followed closely in newspapers, on radio, and on television. All five major political parties are represented in local and federal governments.

The constitution also establishes three branches of government: executive, legislative, and judicial. The executive branch works with the legislative branch to pass and enforce laws. The legislative branch is the Alþing, a one-house lawmaking body. The judicial branch reviews laws and hears trials of people accused of crimes. Iceland's voters elect all members of their government except Supreme Court judges, who are appointed by the president.

Judges of Iceland's Supreme Court

The executive branch is responsible for enforcing Iceland's laws and represents Iceland in international affairs. Iceland's prime minister, cabinet of ministers, and president form the executive branch. The prime minister heads the government. Cabinet ministers are powerful department leaders, usually chosen from the party leading the government. The president represents Iceland at formal events but does not head the government.

The prime minister is not elected in the same way as the president of the United States. The prime minister represents one voting district and is also the leader of a political party. In the federal election, the leader of the party that has the most representatives in the Alþing becomes prime minister.

Currently, no political party has a majority of representatives among the sixty-three-member Alþing. This means that the strongest party forms a union or coalition with another party in order to lead the government. In the 1999 election, for example, the Independence Party and the Progressive Party joined to form the present government. Davíð Oddsson, chairman of the Independence Party, became prime minister. Halldór Ásgrímsson, chairman of the Progressive Party, was appointed minister for the Department of Foreign Affairs and External Trade, the next-highest ministry in the cabinet.

The cabinet is similar to the U.S. cabinet, with departments covering all major areas of Iceland's government. The Foreign-Affairs Department handles relations between Iceland and other countries. Trade and industry, fishery, and agriculture departments look after the business interests of Icelandic

Prime Minister David Oddsson

Prime Minister David Oddsson (1948–) has a distinctive background. He holds a law degree from the University of Iceland and is the chairman of the Independence Party, Iceland's most powerful political group.

Politics are not David's only interests though. He has also been a newspaper reporter, an office manager, and chairman of the Reykjavík Arts Festival. He has written theatrical plays and television dramas, and he has also produced radio programs for the Iceland State Broadcasting Service. David has published one novel, *A Couple of Days Without Gudny*.

companies. The Finance Department oversees collecting taxes and spending money according to the national budget. Other departments include education and culture, justice and religion, communications, environment, health and social security, and social affairs.

Iceland's President

The power of the president of Iceland is more like that of the queen of the United Kingdom than that of the president of the United States. Iceland's president has limited power and does not actually run the country. Instead, the president is a representative of the country, or a figurehead.

The president is elected for a four-year term, but there is no limit to the number of terms a president may serve. Since

Iceland's independence was declared in 1944, the country has had only five presidents.

One of the president's duties is signing laws. Although the president can either sign or veto a law, the power of the veto is limited. If the president vetoes a law, that law is then voted on by Iceland's people, who have the final right of approval or rejection. However, there have been no instances in which the president has vetoed a law passed by the Alþing.

Appointing judges and cabinet ministers is also the president's job. Cabinet appointments are based on the advice of other leaders. The minister of justice and ecclesiastical affairs recommends potential judges to the president for appointment. Although the president appoints cabinet ministers, all candidates are first approved by the prime minister.

The president represents Iceland at official events around the world. The kinds of events that the president might attend include a royal wedding, the Special Olympics, or the funeral of a foreign leader.

Vigdís Finnbogadóttir

Vigdís Finnbogadóttir (1930–) served four terms as president of the Republic of Iceland, from 1980 to 1996. She was the first woman ever elected president of a democratic republic.

In addition to her political career, Vigdís taught French and trained guides for the Icelandic Tourist Bureau. For several years, she directed the Reykjavík Theater Company. Today, she heads the Council of Women World Leaders at the John F. Kennedy School of Government at Harvard University in Massachusetts.

Ólafur Grímsson

Ólafur Ragnar Grímsson (1943–) is a native of Ísafjördur and the current president of Iceland. He is the former chairman of the People's Alliance Party.

Ólafur Grímsson served on the board of the Progressive Party's Youth Federation from 1966 to 1973 and on the Progressive Party's executive board from 1971 to 1973. In 1978, he was elected to the Alþing as a parliamentary member from Reykjavík for the People's Alliance Party. He became leader of the People's Alliance Party in 1987.

Ólafur Grímsson has been active in the International Association of Parliamentarians for Global Action. In

1987, he accepted the Indira Gandhi Peace Prize as representative of that association.

Iceland's National Anthem

"Lofsöngur"
Composed in 1874 by Sveinbjörn Sveinbjörnsson;
lyrics by Matthías Jochumsson

Our country's God! Our country's God!
We worship thy name in its wonder sublime.
The suns of the heavens are set in thy crown
By thy legions, the ages of time!
With thee is each day as a thousand years,
Each thousand of years, but a day.
Eternity's flow'r, with its homage of tears,
That reverently passes away.
Iceland's thousand years!
Eternity's flow'r, with its homage of tears,
That reverently passes away.

The Alþing

According to Iceland's constitution, the Alþing and the president share the responsibility of making laws. The Alþing develops and passes the laws; the president signs the laws. Among the Alþing's many tasks are developing a national budget, passing tax laws, appointing national committee members, and promoting the welfare of Iceland's citizens.

The Alþing is a single-house parliament with sixty-three members who serve terms of up to four years. The number of representatives is decided by a formula that blends population figures and regional interests. Reykjavík has the most representatives, based on its large population. However, small rural regions are guaranteed a minimum of five representatives, regardless of population. In this way, the Alþing balances urban and rural interests.

Members of the Alþing form two basic groups: those in power and those in the opposition. Each group is a combination of at least two political parties. Elections must be held at least every four years, although situations may arise that make an earlier election necessary. If a national crisis occurs or the group in power is not able to pass important laws, the prime minister can call for an election. This election shows the voters' confidence in their government members.

When a new parliament is elected, it first chooses a president. This president is not the president of Iceland, but a leader who helps keep the Alþing moving smoothly. A similar

The Alþing, which makes and passes laws and discusses Icelandic affairs.

NATIONAL GOVERNMENT OF ICELAND

Executive Branch

President		Prime Minister
		Cabinet of Ministers

Legislative Branch

Alþing
(63 members)

Judicial Branch

Supreme Court

District Courts

position in the U.S. government is the Speaker of the House of Representatives. The president of the Alþing presides over meetings but does not usually participate in discussions. In the best sense, the president of the Alþing is like a referee, making sure that all sides of an issue are heard.

Justice for All Icelanders

The Icelandic judicial system works at several different levels. It has ordinary courts, special courts, and an appeals court. In addition to the courts, there are lawyers who represent local or national governments and present cases against accused persons, or defendants.

Ordinary courts deal with civil or criminal issues not handled in the special courts. One judge usually presides over district-court hearings and trials. A typical trial heard at this level might be a lawsuit over a car accident or the trial of a person accused of robbery.

Special courts consist of the Labor Court, the National Court, and the Court of Navigation. The Labor Court deals with problems involving unions and employers' groups. Examples of labor issues brought to court are illegal strikes by union members and the failure of employers to pay employees the wages set down in contracts. The National Court takes over when Parliament decides to prosecute government ministers for committing illegal acts while in office. An example of an issue before the National Court is the misuse of government money; however, there have been no trials in the National Court yet. The Court of Navigation rules over disputes about ship inspections or criminal cases that arise when accidents occur at sea due to navigation errors.

In Iceland, there is only one appeals court—the Supreme Court. Unlike the United States, where there are several levels of appeal in the justice system, Icelanders have only two court opportunities—the original trial and the appeal.

Nine judges sit on the Supreme Court, and all are appointed for life. However, Iceland's judges can retire at age sixty-five, and many choose to do so. New judges are appointed when a justice either dies or retires.

A Handshake at Court

Iceland's Supreme Court has an interesting custom. Before the judges begin work each day, they all shake hands. Why? The handshakes are intended to show that any disagreements or ill feelings from the previous day's work are over, and everyone is facing a new day with a positive attitude.

All nine judges do not preside over every case. Usually three or five judges hear a case brought to the Supreme Court. In very serious situations, seven judges might be asked to preside. The Supreme Court listens to serious civil and criminal appeals. The appeals must be made based on some error in law, such as the failure to follow Iceland's constitution, the failure to uphold a person's civil rights, or an incorrect or overly harsh judgment made in a lower court.

It's the Law

Early laws in Iceland covered every possible event. If a man held his sword a certain way and injured someone, he was punished for that injury. Witchcraft, theft, brawling, and murder received harsh sentences. There were only three punishments for a guilty party: death, exile, and house arrest. While outright murder brought a death sentence, killing a person over an insult was acceptable according to the law. Hurling sand at or punching a person were insults that might end in an acceptable killing.

Modern laws are similar to laws in the United States. Icelanders enjoy the peace and safety of a law-abiding community. Since few policemen spend time chasing criminals in Iceland, they find time for more important things—such as stopping traffic to let a family of ducks cross a road!

Women in Politics

Women take an active part in all aspects of politics in Iceland. At times, Icelandic women have held government offices at all levels, from town mayors to the country's president.

Of the sixty-three members of the Alþing, twenty-two are women. Four women currently serve in the prime minister's cabinet. They are the minister of justice, minister of trade and industry, minister of health and social security, and minister of the environment. One female justice serves on the Supreme Court.

In 1983, a Women's Alliance formed to address women's issues in Iceland, which include child care and equal earning opportunity regardless of gender. Although the Alliance has a large support base, many women in Iceland belong to other political parties, such as the Independence Party or the People's Alliance Party.

Commitment to Its People

Iceland's government is committed to supporting all people, regardless of their ability to earn money. Because of this policy, Iceland is a welfare state. The government plays an important role in social issues, such as health insurance and support for the aged.

Iceland's constitution guarantees that the government will support citizens who are unable to provide for themselves. This includes providing health care, education, retirement pensions, and financial support for food and/or housing. Every Icelandic citizen is covered by state health insurance. The cost of visiting a doctor or staying in the hospital is paid by the government.

The Icelandic Flag

Iceland's flag features a Scandinavian cross in red with a white outline against a field of blue. Blue represents the sea and white stands for the country's glaciers. The red is both a link to Norway and a reminder that the land was forged by volcanic fire.

Not every Icelander wanted this particular flag to fly over Iceland. Many Icelanders preferred another flag, called the Hvítbláinn. Unfortunately, the Hvítbláinn looked a lot like the king of Greece's flag, and the Icelandic government wanted a flag that wouldn't be confused with another country's flag. The current flag, adopted in 1915, flies proudly over Iceland's public buildings today.

Reykjavík: Did You Know This?

Reykjavík lies farther north than any other capital city in the world. It is the business, cultural, and government center of Iceland, as well as the country's largest city. Today, the city and its suburbs account for about 170,000 of Iceland's 286,275 people.

In 1786, Reykjavík became the first settlement in Iceland to be granted town status. At that time, just over 200 people lived in the town. Even as late as 1901, the population was still only 5,000. Growth came to Reykjavík after World War II.

Historically, Reykjavík was the first planned settlement in Iceland. According to legend, Viking Ingólfur Arnarson sailed to Iceland in a longship. He pushed his "high seat" pillars overboard and built his farm where the pillars washed up on the shore. Ingólfur called the place where he settled Reykjavík, meaning "smoky bay," for the steam he saw rising from local hot springs.

As the cultural center of the country, Reykjavík draws Icelanders and tourists to its two major and many smaller theater companies, a national ballet, an

opera company, and the city's many museums. The Einar Jónsson Museum features a sculpture collection by Einar, considered to be one of Iceland's greatest sculptors. The National Gallery displays works by distinguished painter Ásgrímur Jónsson. The Living Art Museum features contemporary works by painters, weavers, sculptors, and experimental artists. The Kjarvalsstaðir Municipal Gallery exhibits the works of Iceland's most famous modern painter, Jóhannes Kjarval, known worldwide for his stunning abstracts.

Music helps Icelanders deal with long, dark winters and enjoy bright summer evenings. Reykjavík houses the national symphony, which features national and international guest artists. If jazz, rock, traditional, or even church music suits your taste, Reykjavík offers the music you want to hear. Idnó, Kaffileikhúsid, and Nordic House all host guest concerts and recitals featuring a variety of musical styles. Hallgrímskirkja, the Lutheran cathedral in Reykjavík, hosts organ recitals on Sundays.

Icelanders love their food, and city restaurants and cafés are kept busy. Seafood restaurants are abundant, but Icelanders also like Italian, Mexican, Chinese, and Thai food. Fast-food fans can stop in at the local burger joints and pizza parlors. However, locals in the know pass by American fast food and head for the Bæjarins bestu hot-dog stand. Decades old, this Reykjavík land-

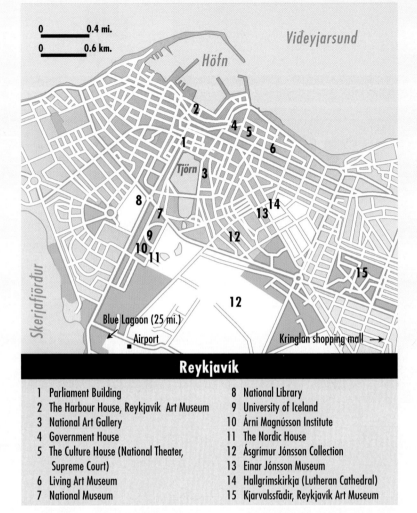

Reykjavík

1 Parliament Building
2 The Harbour House, Reykjavík Art Museum
3 National Art Gallery
4 Government House
5 The Culture House (National Theater, Supreme Court)
6 Living Art Museum
7 National Museum
8 National Library
9 University of Iceland
10 Árni Magnússon Institute
11 The Nordic House
12 Ásgrímur Jónsson Collection
13 Einar Jónsson Museum
14 Hallgrímskirkja (Lutheran Cathedral)
15 Kjarvalssfaðir, Reykjavík Art Museum

mark has people lining up around the block to try its secret-recipe hot dogs.

Iceland's main transportation, business, and industry base is in Reykjavík. The country's dominant industries—fishing and fish processing—provide many jobs for Reykjavík's citizens. Metalworking, textile manufacturing, and shipbuilding employ many other workers. New industries are starting to take hold in Iceland, particularly software development and biotechnology.

CHAPTER

SIX

Harvests from the Sea

ICELAND'S NOBEL PRIZE–WINNING AUTHOR, HALLDÓR Laxness, once claimed that "Life is saltfish." Considering that the country's economic success is tied to fish—fresh, frozen, dried, processed, canned, smoked, and salted—Laxness was probably correct. Fishing provides 70 percent of Iceland's exports and employs about 12 percent of all its workers.

Opposite: **Fishing boats fill an Icelandic harbor.**

Frozen fish awaits export on this freighter.

Weights and Measurements

Iceland uses metric measurements.

For many years, Iceland relied totally on fishing and agriculture for economic survival. In 1960, fish and fish-product exports equaled 90 percent of Iceland's export income. Today, the economy is slowly changing, expanding, and stepping away from its fishing roots. Iceland is developing competitive software, biotechnology, and financial industries.

Cod, Herring, and Caviar

Iceland boasts one of the most technically advanced fishing industries in the world. Helicopters, planes, and radar seek out schools of fish and radio their findings to the fleet. Icelandic fishing ships head out to waters where a successful catch is expected. In order to process and ship fish while it is still fresh, efficiency is a priority. Icelandic fish is in high demand because the island is remote; there is little pollution and cleaner, purer fish.

Icelandic fish and seafood meet a number of market needs. The British prefer cod and haddock—ideal for fish and chips, one of Britain's most popular meals. Germany buys redfish and saithe. To the south, the Spanish, Portuguese, and Italians like salted whitefish. The United States, one of Iceland's largest customers, buys just about anything Icelanders can catch. Gourmet fanciers worldwide enjoy Icelandic smoked salmon, caviar, and sea urchins.

Processing plants turn fish and fish waste into a number of salable products. The largest catch—capelin—provides fish oil and ground fish meal. Waste

Fish are processed on board to ensure freshness.

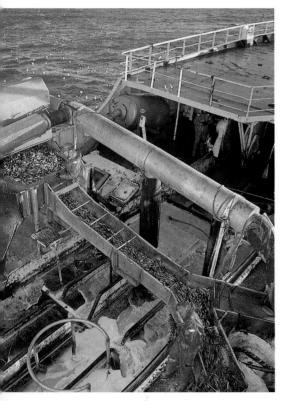

products from most fish are ground into meal and make excellent fertilizer. Iceland's processing plants also turn out large quantities of cod-liver oil, an excellent source of vitamins A and D.

Fish meal and fish oil are Iceland's largest exported marine products, accounting for about 45 percent, or 322,000 metric tons, of exports yearly. Frozen fish comes next at 271,260 metric tons, followed by salted fish and fresh fish.

Thar She Blows!

For many years, whaling was a major industry in Iceland. Whales furnished food, oil for heat, waterproof skin, and bones for meal and fertilizer. However, whaling is a major environmental issue today—one that Icelanders resent. The country's representatives walked out on the International Whaling Commission in 1992. In the ten years that have passed since then, the Commission has been ignored, although Icelandic whaling has not resumed either.

The large number of whales in Icelandic waters creates a problem for fishing vessels. Whales eat fish by the ton and reduce the schools that fishers depend on for income. The country has, however, found a way to turn a "whale" of a profit from these giants of the sea—ecotourism. Whale-watching trips are on the rise in Iceland, providing an excellent profit for only a few hours at sea.

Whale watching has become a prosperous business in Iceland.

What Iceland Grows, Makes, and Mines

Agriculture

Hay	2,338,732 metric tons
Potatoes	9,500 metric tons
Dairy products	105,716 thousand liters
Mutton/lamb	8,176 metric tons

Manufacturing

Aluminum	150,000 metric tons
Cement	117,000 metric tons
Ferrosilicon	61,000 metric tons

Fishing

Capelin	750,066 metric tons
Herring	277,461 metric tons
Cod	242,946 metric tons

A very small percentage of land is used for farming. The sea is the main producer of income for Iceland.

From the Land

When the Vikings settled Iceland, farming and fishing provided everything they needed for survival. Today, Iceland has only about 3,800 working farms, and the number decreases every year. About 5 percent of Iceland's workers farm for a living.

Iceland's major grain crop is hay, grown for feeding live-

stock. Sheep, cattle, and dairy farming provide the bulk of farm income, with most farms raising sheep. The country produces about 8,200 metric tons of mutton and lamb. The dense wool of Icelandic sheep is highly prized in yarn and knit goods. The disease-free Icelandic cattle may well become the beef-of-choice for Europeans concerned about mad cow disease.

Icelanders consume huge quantities of dairy products—the equivalent of 103 gallons (395 l) per person per year. Supermarket dairy departments offer skim, semi-skim, whole, and soured milk; cream; hard and soft cheeses; butter; and plain and flavored yogurt. A dairy delight unique to Iceland is *skyr,* a cross between cottage cheese and yogurt that can be served plain or with fruit.

Food crops grown on Icelandic farms are limited. The major food crop is potatoes, although small quantities of turnips, tomatoes, and cucumbers are also grown. Geothermal hothouses produce bananas, cabbage, lettuce, carrots, and tomatoes, but in amounts too small for commercial use. Most salad greens and fresh vegetables, and practically all fruits, are imported.

This greenhouse worker keeps her plants warm by using geothermal energy.

Renewable Resources

While Iceland has virtually no mineral resources, it has two valuable, renewable resources: freshwater and geothermal energy. Freshwater is essential for fish and food processing, and it also provides abundant hydroelectric power. Iceland has the potential to produce more power than the country needs. In 1998, for example, the nation's electrical use was only 15 percent of its total capacity. At the same time, geothermal energy heated about 85 percent of all residential housing, as well as greenhouses, businesses, and small industries.

Iceland has no oil, gas, iron, coal, or precious-metal deposits so there is no mining. The mass of lava rock does provide some income, however. Iceland exports pumice to Sweden, Denmark, and Norway for making building blocks and chimneys. Pumice also has another use—it is the stone of choice for giving stone-washed denim clothes their "preworn" look!

Manufacturing

Most Icelandic industry is limited to food processing, fish processing, smelting, and building. Aluminum smelting and ferrosilicon production have increased steadily over the past ten years. New smelters continue to be built, expanding aluminum-production capacity.

Construction in Iceland depends heavily on cement. The country's construction industry has found a way to use its plentiful volcanic sand to produce cement and concrete blocks. Most homes, apartment buildings, and businesses are made of cement blocks because wood must be imported.

Iceland's labor force—people aged 16 to 74—totals 167,177 (2000 est.), and 82 percent of them are employed. Unemployment is very low, about 2.7 percent, and reflects the commitment Icelanders have to working. Service industries, such as retail stores, hotels, restaurants, and health services, employ about two-thirds of working Icelanders. These

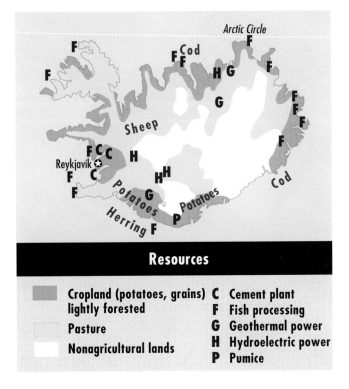

Resources

▓	Cropland (potatoes, grains) lightly forested	C	Cement plant
░	Pasture	F	Fish processing
□	Nonagricultural lands	G	Geothermal power
		H	Hydroelectric power
		P	Pumice

A large majority of Icelanders work in service industries, such as medicine.

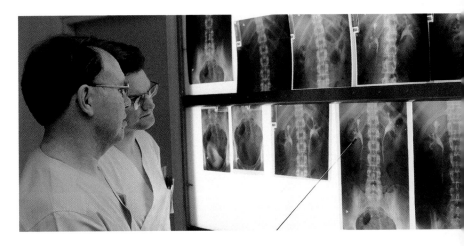

Iceland's Currency

Iceland's currency is the *króna*. The plural of króna is *krónur*. One Icelandic króna equals 100 *aurar*. Icelandic coins come in 5, 10, and 50 aurar and 1, 5, 10, 50, and 100 krónur. Unlike U.S. bills, which are all green, Icelandic krónur bills are printed blue, brown, green, red, yellow, and violet. The bills feature pictures of great Icelandic men and women, such as Jón Sigurdsson and Árni Magnússon, on the front. On the back of each bill is a historic scene honoring the accomplishments of the person pictured on the front. Bills include 10, 50, 100, 500, 1,000, 2,000, and 5,000 krónur.

people work in shops and banks, kitchens and schools, hospitals and offices.

Just over 25 percent of Iceland's employees work in industry. They process fish, make products, construct roads and buildings, and work at power plants. Fishing-industry employees work in both industry and agriculture. People who process fish are considered industrial workers, while those who catch fish are considered agricultural workers.

Salaries are high, with Icelanders among the top earners in Europe. At the same time, Icelanders buy, buy, buy. They own more videotape recorders per person than people in any other country. They also own more cars per person than people anywhere except the United States.

The cost of Iceland's products—milk, meat, and wool, for example—is low. Imported goods, however, are very expensive. Gasoline for cars, fresh fruits and vegetables, and electronic products all carry high price tags.

Let's Go Shopping

Here are common food products in Iceland and their prices:

Product	Price in Icelandic Krónur	Equivalent in U.S.$
Milk, 1 liter	80	0.74
Bread, 1 loaf	125	1.16
Butter, 450 g	180	1.67
Gum, 1 pack	60	0.56
Soda, 2 liters	200	1.86
Cereal, 1 box	250–350	2.32–3.25
Eggs, 1 dozen	250	2.32

Equivalent based on 107.8 Icelandic krónur = U.S.$1, 12/19/01 exchange rate

Strong Viking Stock

WHEN A CHILD IS BORN IN ICELAND, THE NAME CHOSEN for that child is all-important. The child will really have only a first and, perhaps, a middle name. The name usually called a last name, or surname, is, in Iceland, a patronymic—it simply tells who the father is. The patronymic is used to identify which Jón or Inga is being discussed and is not officially a last name. Everyone in Iceland is called by their first name except the bishop and Iceland's president.

Names must be chosen from a government-approved list. Even foreigners who become citizens in Iceland must have Icelandic names. In the 1970s, a number of Vietnamese refugees arrived in Iceland. It is possible that when a man named Phuong Tran, for example, became a citizen, he was given a name like Magnús Árnason. Popular men's names include Þor, Einar, Jón, Magnús, Sigurður, and Helgi. Girls are given names such as Anna, María, Kristín, Guðrún, and Helga.

The patronymic, derived from the father's first name, is used to create a last name. A boy takes his father's first name plus "son." Instead of "son," a girl's patronymic ends in "dóttir." For example, Einar Jónsson has both a son and a daughter. The boy's name is Björn Einarsson, and the girl's name is Kristín Einarsdóttir. Einar's wife's name is Anna Helga Haraldsdóttir, the name she was given at baptism. In Iceland, a woman keeps her name throughout her life, even if she marries. A small percentage of Icelandic families choose to use one last name.

Opposite: **Iceland's future**

The Icelandic Phone Book

Icelandic phone books list people by their first names, followed by their patronymics, addresses, and phone numbers. In a family, each member has a separate listing. Because there are so many duplicate names, phone listings also include the profession of the person listed.

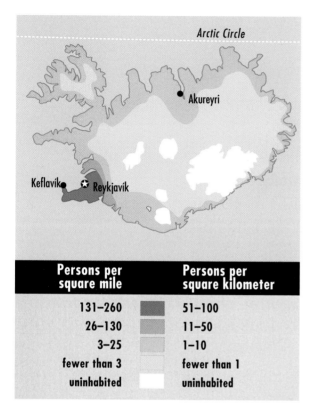

Persons per square mile		Persons per square kilometer
131–260		51–100
26–130		11–50
3–25		1–10
fewer than 3		fewer than 1
uninhabited		uninhabited

A Small Population

Iceland's population is very small for a country—only 286,275 people. For centuries, most Icelanders lived on farms, but this trend changed during the twentieth century. Today, nine out of ten Icelanders live in cities or towns.

The majority of people live in Reykjavík or its suburbs, such as Kópavogur and Hafnarfjörður. In all, the Reykjavík metropolitan area accounts for about 175,000 people, or 61 percent of the county's population. Towns away from the capital area have small populations of fewer than 5,000 people. The one exception is Akureyri, with 15,635 residents.

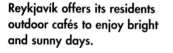

Reykjavík offers its residents outdoor cafés to enjoy bright and sunny days.

Population of Major Cities (2002 est.)

Reykjavík	112,276
Kópavogur	22,587
Hafnarfjörður	19,150
Akureyri	15,635

This girl has the blue eyes and blonde hair of her Norwegian ancestors.

Most of the people who live in Iceland are Icelandic by heritage. For the most part, the people descended from Vikings, and many are blond and blue-eyed, like their Norwegian ancestors. There are some immigrants from Europe and North America. A small Asian group has moved to Iceland although the country as a whole has few minorities.

Chart of Ethnic Groups (2002 est.)

Total Population	286,275
Icelanders	97%
Other Europeans	2%
All Others	1%

Many Icelanders can trace their family lines back over a dozen generations. It is common to hear people talk about someone and mention not only the person's parents, but also his or her grandparents and great-grandparents. Genealogy, the study of families and their ancestors, helps identify exactly which "Árni" or "Guðrún" is being discussed in a country where so many people have the same names.

An island as isolated as Iceland has a small gene pool. Genes are the basic elements of life that determine traits such as height and eye color. When there are few people in a region, such as in Iceland, the low number of available differences in traits creates a small gene pool.

Due to a small gene pool, most Icelanders have similar physical traits.

In 1996, DeCode Genetics, a genetic research company, began mapping the genetic make-up of Icelanders. This idea was met with mixed feelings. Many Icelanders felt DeCode's studies would help Icelanders identify possible medical problems related to genetics. Others considered DeCode's acts a threat to their privacy.

Icelandic Society

Icelanders claim that there is no social class structure in their country. For the most part, this is true. There are minor differences in income, yet every citizen lives on an equal basis. An Icelander's overall approach to life is active and open. Politicians meet regularly with any citizen who makes an appointment. A visit to the prime minister would begin with, "*Góðan dag, Davíð,*" or "Good day, Davíð." Employees call their bosses by their first names and children call their parents, friends, and teachers by their first names.

The extended family—aunts, uncles, cousins, grandparents, and in-laws—are an important part of Icelandic life. For centuries, the entire family worked on a farm and lived together. Since the population has shifted to urban living, extended families no longer live together as they once did. However, family holidays and celebrations are important, and Icelandic families get together for every major holiday.

Being part of the community is an essential part of Icelandic life. Icelanders regularly read one or two local newspapers, attend concerts and plays, and eat out in local restaurants. With such a small population, business, sports, and cultural events couldn't survive without community support.

Icelanders tend to be law-abiding and expect others to be law-abiding too. Until 1995, Iceland had never had a bank robbery. Murder, armed robbery, and other violent crimes are rare. Prison sentences for guilty criminals are shorter than they are in most European or North American countries. A seven-year prison sentence would be the worst sentence any convicted person could expect, and many crimes earn little or no jail time. This country is one of the safest places in the world to live.

The Icelandic Language

People who live in Iceland must learn the language, however. While most Icelanders speak one or more languages, the people take great pride in the purity and history of the Icelandic language. Icelandic today is much as it was during the Settlement Age. As a result, Icelanders can—and do—easily read the sagas in their original twelfth-century forms.

The Icelandic alphabet consists of thirty-six letters. Vowels often have forms, such as *o*, *ó*, and *ö*. Each variation is considered a separate letter. In addition to standard letters, the language has two symbols—*ð* and *þ*—that appear only in Icelandic. The *ð* stands for a soft *th*, as in *mother* or *bother*. A *þ* sounds like a hard *th*, as in *thing* or *thunder*.

Most languages adopt words from other languages. English, for example, relies heavily on Latin and Greek roots, but easily borrows words such as *algebra* (Arabic), *tycoon* (Chinese), *burger* (German), and *rodeo* (Spanish). English has even borrowed one Icelandic word—*geyser*.

This restaurant provides its menu in both English and Icelandic.

This is not true for Icelandic, which tries to use words already in existence rather than borrow from other languages. For example, the Icelandic word for telephone is *simi*—meaning "cord" or "thread." When radios were introduced, they were called *útvarp*, which means "broadcast." Television created a bigger problem and is called *sjónvarp*, literally "sight-cast." Some new Icelandic words show a remarkable sense of humor. Pagers and beepers are called *friðþjófur*—or "thief of the peace."

Rock, River, Glacier

Compound words are common, particularly when describing place names.

Here are some examples:

Term	Meaning	Place Names
Foss	Waterfall	Gullfoss , Dettifoss, Selfoss
Fjörður	Fjord	Ísafjörður, Hvammsfjörður, Vopnafjörður
Jökull	Glacier	Vatnajökull, Hofsjökull, Langjökull
Vatn	Lake	Mývatn, Þingvallavatn
Vík	Bay	Reykjavík, Keflavík, Dalvík

CHAPTER

EIGHT

From Odin to Luther

96

Iceland's Viking settlers believed in powerful gods and goddesses who controlled the future of all people. For them, the world lay beneath the roots of the great tree Yggdrasil, the center of the universe. The mighty Odin, Thor, Balder, Frigg, and other gods lived in Asgard and were called the Aesir. Upon their deaths, Viking warriors hoped to join Odin in Valhalla, the hall of heroes. There, they would train for the final battle at the end of the world.

Another group of gods called the Vanir—Njord, Freya, Freyr, and others—had battled the Aesir. Vikings believed that the Aesir and Vanir reached a truce and lived peacefully—for the time being.

Above: **Yggdrasil tree**
Left: **Freya spinning clouds**

Opposite: **Viking hero Odin**

Norse Gods and Goddesses

	Power or Position
Balder	God of light and peace
Bragi	God of poetry
Freya	Goddess of love and beauty
Freyr	God of fertility
Frigg	Goddess and wife of ruler of the gods
Hel	Giantess of the underworld
Idun	Goddess of immortality
Loki	God of evil and trickery
Njord	God of the sea
Odin	Father or ruler of the gods
Ran	Goddess of the drowned
Skadi	Giantess of the hunt
Thor	God of thunder
Tyr	God of honor, oaths, and truth
Ull	God of archery

The god Thor fights the giants from his chariot.

Besides the gods, there were Norns, dwarfs, and giants. The Norns were three sisters who governed the past, present, and future. They lived at the base of Yggdrasil. Norse dwarfs worked in the mines and fashioned ore into metal. Neither the Norns nor the dwarfs were particularly helpful to the gods and had to be tricked to predict the future or produce weapons for the gods. The giants were the enemies of the gods. In the final battle at the end of the world, mighty tribes of giants would defeat the gods.

Hidden People, Trolls, and Ghosts

Even after Icelanders became Christians, many people believed in folk beings: Hidden People, trolls, and ghosts. Icelandic tales, such as "Glam the Ghost" and "Gryla, the Ogre," continued to be part of the nation's folklore. While most Icelanders don't openly believe in spirits or elves, they allow for the possibility of their existence. Most folk beings can be traced directly to Norse mythology.

There are two stories about how the Hidden People came to be. The first story claims that these elves were children of the Biblical Eve and were hidden from God. God said that they would remain hidden, and so they became the Hidden People. The other story holds that the Hidden People were relatives of the protective spirits of Norse mythology. Either way, there are both good and bad elves. Most Hidden People live under rocks or ledges in rural areas—at least, this is what the folk tales claim.

The Guardian Spirits of Iceland

An Icelandic legend tells of the four guardians (defenders) of the island. Each guardian kept a portion of the country safe. As the story goes, Denmark's king Harald sent a magician to check out Iceland; Harald planned to invade the country.

The magician turned himself into a whale and swam to the island. Along the eastern shore, he met a dragon, along with snakes, worms, and lizards. In the north, a gigantic bird with enormous wings frightened the magician. In the west, a huge bull waded into the water and scared the magician away by snorting and bellowing. Along the southern shore, a mighty giant with an iron rod frightened the magician away.

No matter where he went, the magician could find no easy place to come ashore. In this way, the guardians protected Iceland from the Danish king. Today, Iceland's guardian is the national animal—the seal.

Could this rock be a troll that has turned into stone?

Trolls are distant relatives of the old Norse giants. Trolls are mean-spirited, nasty creatures who cause all kinds of trouble for humans. In the thirteenth century, the tale of Gryla, a mean female ogre, told that Gryla and her husband ate naughty children for dinner. Other legends tell of trolls turning into stone when caught in sunshine. Odd rock formations found throughout Iceland are often credited as being trolls caught by the sun.

Iceland's ghosts are fairly hearty spirits who can either walk as dead people or return to life. Ghosts remain connected to their original bodies, graves, or families. Most are considered evil because of the trouble they are believed to cause. These spirits haunt houses, slam doors, break household goods, or damage roofs.

The Lutheran Church

Since 1550, the Evangelical Lutheran Church has been the state church. About 247,245 Icelanders belong to the Church of Iceland. A large number also belong to a different Lutheran group. In all, about 96 percent of Iceland's people follow Lutheranism. There are also small groups of Seventh-Day Adventists and Roman Catholics.

Hallgrímskirkja

Freedom of religion is guaranteed by Iceland's constitution, which also provides for government-collected taxes for church support. People who choose not to support the church may support the University of Iceland instead.

A bishop leads the Church of Iceland. The church center is at the Hallgrímskirkja. Completed in 1974, the Hallgrímskirkja rises on the eastern end of Lake Tjörn in

Religious Holidays

Epiphany	January 6
Shrove Tuesday	Usually February
Ash Wednesday	Usually February forty days before Easter
Easter Season: Maundy Thursday, Good Friday, Easter Sunday, Easter Monday	March or April
Ascension Day	May 12
Whitsunday, Whitmonday	Forty days after Easter
St. Thorlákur's Day	December 23
Christmas Day	December 25

Saint Thorlákur

December 23 is dedicated to St. Thorlákur, bishop of Skálholt who died on this date in 1193. On this day, Icelanders were originally supposed to fast in honor of their saint. Instead, the day has become a day of feasting on which Icelanders eat cured skate—a type of fish.

The skate can be either buried or hung until it is cured. The fish is soaked, then boiled for ten minutes. On St. Thorlákur's Day, skate is served with lamb fat.

Reykjavík. Lutherans follow the basic ideas set forth by Martin Luther in the early 1500s. They believe that grace comes through faith, and they follow the teachings of the Bible. Lutherans practice three main sacraments: penance, baptism, and communion.

Although many Icelanders are not active churchgoers, religious holidays are popular. Shrove Tuesday, the day before Lent begins, is called Sprengidagur and is celebrated by eating pea soup and salted mutton. Ash Wednesday gives children a chance to act out. The children tie small bags of ashes on their backs, and they spend much of the day collecting money for sweets and treats.

Easter is a family time. Confirmation is usually scheduled for teenagers around Easter. School and offices close for five days—from Holy Thursday through Easter Monday. Families usually take this time to travel and visit relatives, particularly if Easter falls in April, and spring is well on the way.

The Christmas season in Iceland stretches over thirteen days, from dusk on Christmas Eve to January 6, the Feast of the Epiphany or Þrettándinn. Christmas celebrations include traditional foods, a tree, and gifts. Hangikjöt (smoked mutton) and rjúpa (roasted ptarmigan) make up the main course for Christmas dinner. There are also cookies, cakes with whipped cream, and laufabraud (fried bread carved with decorations).

Christmas Eve brings a special thrill for children. The family eats dinner and listens to Christmas songs on the radio. Once dinner is over, presents are opened. For the thirteen days between Christmas and Epiphany, children will be on the lookout for special gifts left by the Yuletide Lads. According to Icelandic tradition, naughty children get a potato instead of a present.

Christmas Day is a family day with more feasting and sweets. Winter months have very little sunshine, but Icelandic families brighten the holiday season with Christmas lights and decorations.

Christmas season begins with the lighting of the tree.

Jólasveinarnir, "The Yuletide Lads"

The Yuletide Lads are the thirteen sons of Gryla the ogre, and a rowdier group of tricksters would be hard to find.

Each lad is named for the particular type of prank he pulls. Gluggagægir, "Window Peeper," peeks in windows and steals what he sees. Skyrgámur, "Curd Glutton," sneaks into kitchens and gobbles up all the skyr, a dairy food. When the Yuletide Lads first became popular in the 1600s, they were mischief-makers who played nasty tricks on people throughout the thirteen-day Christmas season. Today, they leave little presents in children's shoes.

Icelanders: Indoors and Out

THE WRITTEN WORD HOLDS AN IMPORTANT PLACE IN Iceland's society. One out of ten Icelanders writes and publishes a book during his or her lifetime. Iceland prints and sells more books per person than any other country.

In Iceland, a book helps fill dark winter days. Books are popular presents for birthdays, weddings, and most other life events. Every family has a library in which poetry and great works of literature stand on shelves beside science-fiction novels and historic tales.

Opposite: **A bookstore in Iceland displays the wealth of books available to its citizens.**

A special part of the day is when a mother can read to her child.

The *Edda* and the saga were the first works of literature in Iceland. Written during the Age of Writing (1120–1230), these epic poems retold the adventures of daring, fearless men and women. *Njal's Saga* is perhaps the best-known family saga. This story has all the stuff of which modern movies are made: best friends caught in a feud between quarreling wives, good against evil, wisdom, fighting, cunning, revenge, and a handful of killings thrown in for spice. Njal and all his sons die, but Njal's son-in-law Kari eventually brings the feud to an end.

Saving Iceland's Heritage

In 1702, Árni Magnússon (1663–1730) traveled from Denmark to his native Iceland to conduct a census. Fascinated by the ancient sagas, Árni began collecting original saga documents. He spent most of his adult life collecting and copying sagas and preserving the literary heritage of Iceland. In 1728, a fire destroyed part of Árni's collection. He was heartbroken at the loss. He died two years later. He left his collection to the University of Copenhagen. It was not until the 1960s that Denmark began returning Árni's collection to Iceland (pictured). This event brought a close to Iceland's colonial connection and restored a priceless gift to Iceland's people.

Through the sagas, readers learn about Viking life. They witness violent struggles between powerful chieftains, as well as battles of wits between the clever and the not-so-clever. They learn how simple games and parties could lead to deadly battles. The ideals of honor, loyalty, and courage are represented beside envy, greed, and bloated pride.

When the Age of Writing ended, Icelandic writers continued their interest in poetry. Poets enjoyed creating an exciting new form of epic poetry called *rimur* and of religious poetry, such as *Lilja* by Eysteinn Ásgrímsson.

Between 1400 and 1800, Iceland's loss of independence, along with its poverty and isolation, made an impact on its literature. Icelanders turned to stories and poems about famous heroes and great deeds to overcome daily hardships.

In the 1800s, poet Jónas Hallgrímsson changed Icelandic poetry forever. Jónas Hallgrímsson was a multitalented man— a poet and a scientist. Many consider him Iceland's greatest poet. Jónas's poetry described the Icelandic people and the country's stark beauty in a way that brought new pride to Icelanders and a new writing style to Icelandic literature.

The Modern Icelandic Novel

The first Icelandic novel, *A Boy and A Girl* by Jón Þóroddsen, appeared in 1850. The concept of novel writing was new to Iceland, but the literary form followed the traditions of the great sagas: exciting characters and gripping plot lines set against the rugged background of Iceland.

Halldór Kiljan Laxness

Having written over sixty novels and plays, Halldór Laxness (1902–1998) was Iceland's leading author of the twentieth century. Halldór completed his first book at age seventeen, then left Iceland to explore Europe. After he converted to Catholicism as a young man, his writing leaned toward his newly found religious views.

Later in life, Halldór Laxness chose the Icelandic people and their daily lives as main topics for his novels. He also produced historical novels, influenced by Iceland's sagas. His books continue to be read by thousands of Icelanders, and college students study his novels. One of his most famous novels is *The Fish Can Sing*.

By the beginning of the twentieth century, the novel had taken hold. New writers, such as Þorgils Gjallandi and Gunnar Gunnarsson, studied the popular foreign writers of the time. Their writing styles were realistic and modern. Some, like Gunnar Gunnarsson, wrote in Danish or Norwegian. However, the works had an obvious Icelandic influence and are considered Icelandic regardless of the language in which they were written.

By the mid-1900s, writing and publishing had become an Icelandic passion. New writers penned short stories and novels almost as quickly as publishers could get the works into print. The most important writer of the time was Halldór Kiljan Laxness, the first Icelandic writer to win the Nobel Prize for Literature. His work reflects the daily lives of Icelanders from all walks of life.

Icelandic Art

Painting and sculpture did not become popular in Iceland until the early 1900s. The country's first landscape artist, Ásgrímur Jónsson (1876–1958), followed the Impressionist style of painting. His watercolors are on display in his Reykjavík home and studio, which is now the Ásgrímur Jónsson Museum.

While landscapes have some popularity, city life is the source of inspiration for modern artists. For Thorvaldur Skúlason (1906–1984), for example, city scenes and Icelandic fishing life were the main themes.

Ásgrímur Jónsson Museum

Iceland's best-known artist is Jóhannes Kjarval (1885–1972), who painted modern abstract pieces. Jóhannes studied art in England and was influenced by English painters of the late 1800s and early 1900s. One of his most common themes is the spirit beings inhabiting Iceland's lava rocks.

Sculpture in Iceland is growing in popularity. The country's first prominent sculptor was Einar Jónsson (1874–1954) who used Saga Age themes in his early work, although most

Utlaginn, "The Outlaw," sculpted by Einar Jónsson

of his work is modern. Today, the works of Icelandic sculptors are featured in Reykjavík's Ásmundur Sveinsson Sculpture Gallery and in the Einar Jónsson Museum.

Modern Icelandic sculpture on display

Icelandic Symphony Orchestra

Most performing arts are presented in Reykjavík, Iceland's cultural center. The Icelandic Symphony Orchestra's weekly concerts feature guest conductors and performers from all over the world. Icelandic composer Jón Leifs's music is often played at symphony concerts.

Iceland's opera company performs before a small but loyal audience. The opera house only seats 400, but is usually filled to capacity. Operas by Richard Wagner—many with Norse themes—draw standing-room-only audiences.

Popular music in Iceland comes mostly from Europe and the United States with one major exception: Björk. This talented Icelander has several gold and platinum albums, including *Debut* and *Life's Too Good* (as a member of the Sugarcubes).

Music is a regular part of Icelandic daily life. Iceland's many nightclubs feature live bands playing popular music to jazz. Just about every town has a mixed chorus that performs on major holidays and gives public concerts. Folk, classical, and church music concerts are held weekly during the summer months. Every other year, Reykjavík holds a jazz festival, that draws jazz musicians and singers from around the world.

Iceland also has its own film industry. Its leading filmmaker is Fridrik Thór Fridriksson, whose film *Children of Nature* was nominated for an Academy Award.

Indoors and Outdoors

Long, dark winters have encouraged Icelanders to play indoor sports and

Björk

Iceland's best-known musician, Björk Guðmundsdóttir has become one of pop culture's biggest stars. Björk, born in Reykjavík on November 21, 1965, released her first album when she was eleven years old. She toured with the Sugarcubes for several years before going solo in 1992. Despite worldwide fame, Björk always enjoys returning to her homeland.

games. Chess and games that promote physical fitness, such as handball, help to fill their time.

Chess is a favorite game for sharpening the mind. Iceland proudly boasts of its six chess grand masters, the highest achievement for a chess player. This number is quite high for a country with such a small population. However, chess fills many long winters with sharp strategies and hard-fought battles. Chess clubs are found throughout the country, and the Icelandic National Chess Championship is fiercely contested.

These boys ponder their next moves in a good game of chess.

Glíma

Two men, Helgi and Árni, study each other across an open mat. Helgi, the audience favorite, often wins his matches. The men dodge and weave, looking for an advantage. Suddenly, Helgi leaps at his opponent. He grabs Árni's pants and lifts him high into the air. Árni struggles but cannot defeat the stronger Helgi. Árni is thrown to the mat, and Helgi wins again. The sport is glíma, the Viking form of wrestling.

Handball, basketball, and indoor swimming keep Icelandic bodies fit and trim throughout the long winters. Handball's popularity in Iceland comes from being fast paced and competitive. Also, it can be played on indoor courts. Aerobics and weight lifting keep city gyms busy every night.

Icelandic federal law prohibits boxing because it is considered too violent. Instead, most Icelanders prefer *glíma*—the country's national sport and the ancient Viking form of wrestling.

Above left: **Margret Olafsdóttir**

Above right: **Rakel Karvelsson**

Soccer is Iceland's most popular team sport, with children beginning to play in elementary school. Professional soccer draws big crowds to the stadium in Reykjavík for local and international matches. Icelandic players, called footballers, sometimes play for clubs in other European countries.

Women also play international-level soccer, competing in the Women's World Cup competition. Two Icelandic national teammates—Margret Olafsdóttir and Rakel Karvelsson—played in the 2001 season of the Women's United Soccer Association on the Philadelphia team.

Once snow falls, cross-country and downhill skiing draw many Icelanders to the slopes. The skiing there is not as exciting as skiing in the Swiss Alps, but there is plenty of snow. Nearer home, children sled and skate; they also have snowball fights, just like North American children.

Although Iceland's climate and landscape do not lend themselves to golf, there are golf courses and an international golf tournament. Called the Arctic Open, the tournament is played at Akureyri's golf course in June, when the sun never sinks below the horizon. The tournament begins at midnight and runs until the wee hours of the morning.

During the summer months Icelanders head for pools, hiking trails, and wilderness camping sites.

Learning to skate is common during the winter months in Iceland.

The Heart of Iceland: Family

From the day they're born until the day they die, Icelanders are wrapped in the arms of their families. Families spend their holidays, feasts, and vacations together, and a "family" includes grandparents and great-grandparents, as well as aunts, uncles, and cousins.

Newborn babies join a long, rich heritage in Iceland. A newborn baby's name is usually not revealed until the child is baptized. This tradition dates back to days when children rarely lived beyond their first birthdays. Today, Iceland has one of the lowest infant-death rates in the world, yet the tradition continues.

A child is often named after his or her grandparents. Again, this tradition stretches back to a time when it was rare for a grandparent to still be alive when a new member joined the family. With today's lengthy life spans, many Icelandic children have both grandparents and great-grandparents when they are born.

Weddings bring families together again. The groom and his best man sit at the front of the church on the right side of the aisle. The bride and her father sit

Opposite: **Family time is important to the people of Iceland.**

A traditional wedding allows two families to come together.

to the left. As guests enter the church, the groom and best man bow. Entering male guests bow in return, and some women curtsy.

After the marriage ceremony, the groom joins his new wife on her side of the church to show that the bride's family will always be important to the couple. The bride's father then joins the groom's father on the groom's side of the church, showing the link between the two families.

Knee Breeches and Tall Caps

Traditional dress in Iceland reminds people of clothes worn in the 1800s. The women wear black home-spun skirts and black, long-sleeved jackets that button to the neck. The clothes feature rich gold or bright-colored embroidery. A gold belt around the waist completes the outfit. On their heads, women wear tall white caps.

Men traditionally wear dark knee breeches, high socks, and jackets with two rows of brass buttons down the front. Men's knit caps are made of wool and dyed with herbs.

The strength of family extends to the loss of one of its members. An Icelandic family may prefer to have the coffin kept in a chapel or in the home. A few days after a death, there is a coffin-closing ceremony for family members only. Although many people choose to have a church funeral service, the family may want to conduct the funeral themselves instead of having a minister.

In Iceland, every death is significant, and the life of each person who dies is honored with a full-page obituary in the local newspaper. The person's life and accomplishments fill the page. In addition, close friends write short articles about the importance of the deceased. Some famous Icelanders have obituaries as long as three or four pages.

When the burial service is over, the deceased person is not forgotten. The family returns at Christmas each year to place candles and pine bows on the grave. Many Icelanders place flowers on the grave on the deceased's birthday, too. Since one or more of the grandchildren have probably been named in the deceased's honor, memories of those who have died continue through the family line.

Celebrating Holidays

The year begins with a New Year's Eve celebration. In every town, bonfires light up the night skies. In Icelandic folklore, New Year's Eve was a time when cows spoke, seals became human, and elves made

National Holidays

New Year's Day	January 1
Maundy Thursday, Good Friday, Easter Sunday and Monday	March or April
First Day of Summer	Third Thursday of April
Labor Day	May 1
Independence Day	June 17
Businessmen's Holiday Weekend	First weekend in August
Christmas	December 25
Boxing Day	December 26

New Year's fireworks light
the night sky.

mischief around the house. Today, New Year's Eve is a community celebration, and families join one another to watch dazzling fireworks light up the dark winter skies.

Weekdays—Old and New

In the Old Icelandic language, names of weekdays resembled the names used in English. For example, Monday was Mánadagur, and Thursday was Tórsdagur. In Iceland today, some days are named for their order in the week. Monday, Saturday, and Sunday kept their Old Icelandic names, but days in the middle of the week changed entirely. Tuesday is named Þridjudagur, meaning "third day," and Thursday is named Fimmtudagur, or "fifth day." Wednesday takes the name Midvikudagur, or "middle-of-the-week day."

Most public holidays are either connected to the nation's history, such as Independence Day, or to religious events. However, Icelanders never forget their ties to their Viking heritage, the sea, and the land.

Many Viking customs are still part of the Icelandic family's year. One such event is Þorrablót, held in February. Each year, Icelanders hail the passing of another winter by celebrating Þorrablót. Foods that once made the difference between survival and starvation are now served at classic Þorrablót feasts. Buffet tables groan under the weight of dried fish, cured shark meat, lamb sausages, and *svið*.

Summer brings a tribute to all seamen on Sjómannadagur, or Seaman's Day. Icelanders gather for parades, races, tugs-of-war, and sea-rescue competitions. Because so many Icelanders make their livings on the sea, swimming, rowing, and lifesaving are respected skills. People of all ages show off their sea-linked abilities on Seaman's Day.

Svið

Svið is a boiled sheep's head. The head is dipped in hot oil to singe off the wool. The skull is cut in two and boiled. The dish is served either hot or pickled.

A rescue simulation is performed on Seaman's Day.

Bun Day

Icelandic children cannot wait until Bolludagur, or "Bun Day," arrives. On this winter holiday, children wake early and race to their parents' bedrooms with their "bun wands," decorated with colorful paper and ribbons. Children earn one bun for every tap with the wand needed to rouse their sleepy parents. The buns are filled with jam or whipped cream and are often topped with chocolate.

Dining à la Iceland

Icelanders happily consume burgers, hot dogs, and pizza. They dine out on Indian curry, Italian lasagna, and Mexican tacos. When they eat at home, the food served is simple.

Most Icelandic homemade dinners consist of boiled fish (haddock or cod), potatoes, and some kind of cabbage, green bean, or pea dish. On farms, lamb is the meat most often served, and it may be roasted, salted, or smoked. Dried or salted fish is sold in most grocery stores. Dried fish is eaten much like beef jerky. Bite it and chew.

Wheat is not grown in Iceland, so while wheat bread is available, it is not usually served at home. Instead, rye bread is the everyday bread of Iceland and accompanies most meals.

Typical vegetables served with a meal are cabbage, onions, and perhaps, various forms of seaweed. Most Icelanders serve potatoes at home but might not have a green vegetable

A family enjoys a home-cooked meal together.

Icelandic Crêpes

Yield: twelve to fourteen 3-inch pancakes

Ingredients

- 1 cup flour
- 1/2 teaspoon baking soda
- 1 egg, beaten
- 1 teaspoon sugar
- 1 1/2–2 cups milk
- 2 tablespoons melted butter or margarine

Beat egg in a small bowl. In a large mixing bowl, blend all ingredients thoroughly. Batter will be smooth and thin. Spray griddle with butter-flavored nonstick spray. Pour about 2 tablespoons of batter on hot griddle. Brown on both sides, turning each crêpe over when air bubbles burst on top. Serve with brown sugar or covered in jam.

because fresh vegetables and fruits are generally imported. Although tomatoes, cucumbers, and lettuce are grown in hothouses, not enough salad vegetables are produced to bring prices down.

Education

Every Icelandic child begins school at age seven and continues until age sixteen. School is divided into primary or elementary schools; junior high; secondary or high schools; and college or university.

Children learn reading, math, science, social studies, and language arts. In fourth grade they begin studying Danish, and English study starts in sixth grade. Every child must learn how to swim as part of the school program.

When students finish ninth grade (at age sixteen), they may leave school or go on for higher education. High schools are called grammar or comprehensive schools, and there are also a number of vocational or trade schools. Grammar-school students are seventeen to twenty years old.

Vocational or trade schools teach skills needed in the workplace. Iceland has a technical school, a school of business, and an agricultural college. Students at these institutions train for positions in banks, offices, mechanics' workshops, and on farms. They might also learn plumbing, carpentry, or electrical trades.

Iceland recognizes the need for artists to develop their talents. Reykjavík has a drama academy, a musical school, and the Icelandic College of Arts and Crafts. Students must audition before gaining acceptance to these specialized colleges.

The University of Iceland and the University of Akureyri, the country's two universities, offer standard courses of study. Most courses are taught in Icelandic, although English is spoken in a number of classes.

Icelandic teens are encouraged to have part-time jobs. They earn money after school and on weekends or work during vacations. In the summer months, many urban Icelandic teenagers work on their relatives' farms. There, young Icelanders learn to appreciate the demands of dawn-to-dusk farmwork.

These Icelandic youngsters spend their summers on the family farm.

Timeline

Iceland's History

Irish explorers land on Iceland.	A.D. 800
First settlers from Norway arrive. Reykjavík is founded.	874
Alþing, the first government meets.	930
Christianity is adopted. Leif "the Lucky" Eiríksson discovers North America.	1000
Icelandic sagas are written.	1120–1230
Norway begins ruling Iceland.	1262
Norway and Iceland unite with Denmark.	1380
The Black Death kills many Icelanders.	1402–1404
Árni Magnússon collects sagas.	Early 1700s
Laki Volcano erupts in the worst eruption in Icelandic history.	1783–1786
Reykjavík gains town status and trade rights.	1786

World History

2500 B.C.	Egyptians build the Pyramids and the Sphinx in Giza.
563 B.C.	The Buddha is born in India.
A.D. 313	The Roman emperor Constantine recognizes Christianity.
610	The Prophet Muhammad begins preaching a new religion called Islam.
1054	The Eastern (Orthodox) and Western (Roman) Churches break apart.
1066	William the Conqueror defeats the English in the Battle of Hastings.
1095	Pope Urban II proclaims the First Crusade.
1215	King John seals the Magna Carta.
1300s	The Renaissance begins in Italy.
1347	The Black Death sweeps through Europe.
1453	Ottoman Turks capture Constantinople, conquering the Byzantine Empire.
1492	Columbus arrives in North America.
1500s	The Reformation leads to the birth of Protestantism.
1776	The Declaration of Independence is signed.
1789	The French Revolution begins.

Iceland's History

Alþing is dissolved.	**1800**
Iceland gets a new constitution.	**1874**
Iceland achieves home rule under Denmark.	**1904**
Icelandic women are granted the right to vote.	**1917**
Denmark recognizes Iceland as a separate state.	**1918**
British troops occupy Iceland in World War II.	**1940**
Iceland declares independence at Þingvellir.	**1944**
Iceland joins the United Nations.	**1946**
Surtsey, a new island, is formed off Iceland's coast.	**1963**
Helgafell erupts, destroying many houses on Heimaey.	**1973**
Fishery limits expand to 200 miles (300 km).	**1975**
Iceland has "Cod War" with Britain.	**1976**
Vigdís Finnbogadóttir becomes the first woman elected president of a republic.	**1980**
U.S. president Ronald Reagan and Soviet premier Mikhail Gorbachev hold summit meetings in Reykjavík.	**1986**
Iceland walks out on the International Whaling Commission, although whaling in Iceland stops.	**1992**
Avalanches kill thirty-four people in the West Fjords.	**1995**
Return of Árni Magnússon saga collection is completed.	**1997**
Volcanic activity under the Vatnajökull produces meltwater that floods southeastern Iceland.	**2001**

World History

1865	The American Civil War ends.
1914	World War I breaks out.
1917	The Bolshevik Revolution brings communism to Russia.
1929	Worldwide economic depression begins.
1939	World War II begins, following the German invasion of Poland.
1945	World War II ends.
1957	The Vietnam War starts.
1969	Humans land on the moon.
1975	The Vietnam War ends.
1979	Soviet Union invades Afghanistan.
1983	Drought and famine in Africa.
1989	The Berlin Wall is torn down, as communism crumbles in Eastern Europe.
1991	Soviet Union breaks into separate states.
1992	Bill Clinton is elected U.S. president.
2000	George W. Bush is elected U.S. president.

Fast Facts

Official name:	Republic of Iceland
Capital:	Reykjavík
Official language:	Icelandic
Religion:	Lutheranism, 96 percent

Reykjavík

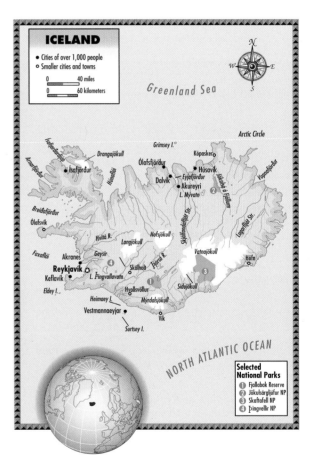

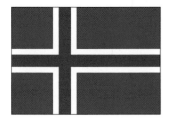

Iceland's flag

Rock formation

First civilization on Iceland:	A.D. 874, Norwegian settlement
National anthem:	"Lofsöngur," words by Matthías Jochumsson, music by Sveinbjörn Sveinbjörnsson
Government:	Constitutional Republic
Chief of state:	President
Head of government:	Prime Minister
Independence:	June 17, 1944
Area:	39,756 square miles (103,000 sq km)
Highest elevation:	Hvannadalshnúkur, 6,952 feet (2,119 m)
Lowest elevation:	Sea level along the coast
Longest river:	Þjórsá, 144 miles (230 km)
Largest glacier:	Vatnajökull, 3,200 square miles (8,300 sq km)
Greatest distance east to west:	300 miles (483 km)
Greatest distance north to south:	190 miles (306 km)
Largest lake:	Þingvallavatn, 32 square miles (83 sq km)
Average annual precipitation:	Reykjavík, 31.5 inches (80.5 cm)
Length of coastline:	3,137 miles (4,988 km)
Average July temperature:	Reykjavík, 52°F (11°C)
Lowest recorded temperature:	−36°F (−37.9°C) Grímstadir, January 1918

Þingvellir

Currency

National population (2002 est.):	286,275	
Ethnic groups:	Icelanders	97 percent
	Europeans	2 percent
	Other	1 percent
Population in major cities (2002 est.):	Reykjavík	112,276
	Kópavogur	22,587
	Hafnarfjörður	19,150
	Akureyri	15,635

Population density: 6.5 people per square mile (2.5 people per sq km)

Population distribution: 92 percent urban, 8 percent rural

Famous landmarks:
- ▶ *Lake Mývatn*
- ▶ *Krafla Volcano*
- ▶ *Vatnajökull*
- ▶ *Skaftafell National Park*
- ▶ *Jökulsárgljúfur National Park*
- ▶ *Vestmannaeyjar (Westman Islands)*
- ▶ *Gullfoss and Great Geysir*
- ▶ *Blue Lagoon*

Industry: Manufacturing: fish processing, pumice, concrete, wool. Agriculture: potatoes, turnips, sheep, hens, dairy products. Fish and seafood: cod, redfish, haddock, herring, capelin, shrimp.

Currency: 1 Icelandic króna= 100 aurar

Currency exchange: 107.8 krónur = U.S.$1 [12/29/01]

System of weights and measures: Metric system

Icelandic children

Vigdís Finnbogadóttir

Literacy rate: 99.9 percent

Common Icelandic words and phrases:

Góðan dag	Hello or good morning
Gott kvöld	Good evening
Ég heiti…	My name is …
Hvað segirðu got?	How are you?
Bless	Goodbye
Já	Yes
Nei	No
Takk	Thanks
Má eg fá…?	May I have…?
Ég skil ekki.	I do not understand.

Famous Icelanders:

Bishop Jón Arason of Hólar (1484–1550)
Clergyman who brought the printing press to Iceland in 1530

Ingólfur Arnarson (874–)
First permanent settler

Vigdís Finnbogadóttir (1930–)
First elected woman president of a democratic republic

Ólafur Grímsson (1943–)
Fifth president of the Republic of Iceland

Björk Guðmundsdóttir (1965–)
Popular singer known as Björk

Jónas Hallgrímsson (1807–45)
Best-loved Icelandic national poet

Halldór Laxness (1902–1998)
Nobel Prize-winning author

Jón Sigurðsson (1811–1879)
Leader of the independence movement and national hero

Snorri Sturluson (1179–1241)
Premier writer of Icelandic sagas

Sveinbjörn Sveinbjörnsson (1847–1922)
Musician and composer of Iceland's national anthem

To Find Out More

Nonfiction

▶ Byock, Jesse L. ed. *The Saga of the Volsungs: The Norse Epic of Sigurd the Dragon Slayer*. New York: Penguin, 2000.

▶ Philip, Neil. *Odin's Family: Myths of the Vikings*. New York: Orchard Books, 1996.

▶ Pitkänen, Matti A. *The Grandchildren of the Vikings*. Minneapolis: Carolrhoda Books, Inc., 1996.

▶ Stefoff, Rebecca. *The Viking Explorers*. Broomall, PA: Chelsea House, 1993.

▶ Wilcox, Jonathan. *Iceland*. Tarrytown, NY: Marshall Cavendish, 1996.

▶ Fiction

Wisniewski, David. *Elfwyn's Saga*. New York: Lothrop, 1990.

Music

▶ Islandica. *Songs & Dances from Iceland*. Arc, 1994.

Web Sites

▶ **Alþing of Iceland**
http://www.althingi.is
Official site of the Icelandic legislature, includes information about Parliament House and the workings of the Alþing.

▶ **Embassy of Iceland**
http://www.iceland.org
General information on Iceland.

▶ **Icelandic Tourist Bureau**
http://www.goiceland.org
Tourist information, history, and government material, as well as facts about key cities.

Videotapes

▶ *Iceland: Europe's Outback.* Director: Rick Ray. ASIN: 1879587017.

▶ *The Turtle Expedition Explores Iceland: Land of Fire and Ice.* Director: Frank Kemp. ASIN: B00005A7JJ.

▶ *Volcano!* Director: Aram Boyajian. National Geographic Video, 1990.

Organizations and Embassies

▶ **Embassy of Iceland**
1156 15th Street, NW, Suite 1200
Washington, DC 20005-1704

▶ **Iceland Tourist Office**
655 Third Avenue
New York, NY 10017

▶ **National Archives of Iceland**
Laugavegur 162
105 Reykjavík, Iceland

▶ **Office of the President**
Sóleyjargötu 1
IS-150 Reykjavík, Iceland

▶ **Trade Council of Iceland**
P. O Box 1000
IS-121 Reykjavík, Iceland

Index

Page numbers in *italics* indicate illustrations.

Meet the Author

BARBARA A. SOMERVILL considers herself a "life-long learner." She feels that every day is a chance to find out about different people, places, and ideas. Many of her writing assignments prove to be learning opportunities, and researching this book about Iceland fascinated her.

Barbara's interest in different places began as a young child. Her family traveled by car each year from New York to Florida. She vividly remembers one trip when the family traveled the Blue Ridge Parkway, giving her a taste of the Appalachian Mountains. Since those days, she has traveled to every state except Alaska—although that's definitely on her list of places to go.

She has also lived in Canada and Australia, which gave Barbara an appreciation of different cultures. When she travels to new places now, she avoids the typical tourist sites and tries to do things local people do. One thing is sure—she never eats American fast food when out of the United States. Eating like the locals gives her a sense of living in the place.

Barbara's writing career began when she first picked up a pencil—although she has used her writing in many different

ways. At times, she has been a language-arts teacher, an investigative reporter, a corporate writer, an advertising copywriter, a journalist, and an author. She has written more than a dozen children's textbooks and nonfiction books, about one hundred video scripts, and several hundred magazine articles. The strangest topics she has ever written about are cowboy hats, coffins, and how to retread truck tires.

She says the challenge of children's nonfiction writing is to make a topic come alive, yet pack in enough details and facts to make the book informative. Barbara takes advantage of her local library system and the Internet to do research. For this book, she sent e-mails to a number of Icelanders—all of whom responded with interest.

Barbara Somervill was born in New Rochelle, New York. She has also lived in Toronto (Canada), Canberra (Australia), Palo Alto (California), and South Carolina. She reads, loves movies and theater, and plays duplicate bridge. She is the mother of four sons—all adults—and the grandmother of one delightful little girl.

Photo Credits

Photographs © 2002:

A Perfect Exposure: 7 bottom, 10, 19, 27, 29 top, 29 bottom, 39, 43, 45, 76, 78, 91, 101,130, 132 top (Randa Bishop), 12, 41, 58, 64, 66, 74, 109, 114, 125 (Inger Helene Boasson/ NordicPhotos), 120 (Palmi Guomundsson/NordicPhotos), 73 (Thorsten Henn/NordicPhotos), 8, 9, 31, 57, 70, 71, 85, 88, 92, 105, 110, 112, 117, 119, 122, 133 bottom, 133 top (Bragi Josefsson), 123 (Oddgeir Karlsson/NordicPhotos), 124 (Kristjan Maack/NordicPhotos), 11 (NordicPhotos), 115 (NordicPhotos/ DV), 86 bottom, 86 top, 132 bottom (NordicPhotos/SSJ), 23, 95 (Richard T. Nowitz), 81 (Jon Vior Sigurosson/ NordicPhotos), 14, 15, 18, 22, 24, 26, 30, 35, 40, 65, 79, 80, 82, 90, 100, 103, 131 (Haukur Snorrason)

AKG London: 96

AllSport USA/Getty Images: 116 top right (Tony Quinn), 116 top left (Chris Stanford)

AP/Wide World Photos/Jacques Brinon: 113

Art Resource, NY/Werner Forman: 51

Bridgeman Art Library International Ltd., London/New York: 47, 97 top

Corbis Images: 46, 50 bottom (Paul Almasy), 20 top, 50 top (Bettmann), 83, 111 (Dave G. Houser), 2, 84, 104, 106, 108 (Bob Krist), 42 (Melvyn P. Lawes), 36 bottom (Joe McDonald), 68 (Reuters NewMedia Inc.), 127 (Ted Spiegel), 63 (Peter Turnley), cover, 6, 25, (Brian Vikander), 118 (Nik Wheeler), 38 (Winifred Wisniewski), 33 (Lawson Wood), 69 (Inge Yspeert)

Getty Images: 48 (Luis Castaneda Inc.), 34 (Anders Geidemark), 7 top, 32 (Art Wolfe)

Hulton | Archive/Getty Images: 20 bottom (Liaison Agency), 60

Mary Evans Picture Library: 53, 97 bottom, 98

National Museum of Iceland: 61

The Image Works/Topham: 36 top

Maps by Joe LeMonnier